TALES FROM THE IVORY TOWER

About the Author

Jim Malone is the Robert Boyle Professor (Emeritus) of Medical Physics at Trinity College Dublin and was Dean of its School of Medicine. He has a life-long interest in the arts, literature, religious studies, music and set-dancing, and was a regular participant in Merriman Summer Schools, directing two. He retired early and explored new horizons, during which he completed an MA on personal spiritualities. He is regularly retained as a consultant by international organisations including the International Atomic Energy Agency and the World Health Organisation.

TALES FROM THE IVORY TOWER

Jim Malone

The Liffey Press

Published by
The Liffey Press Ltd
'Clareville'
307 Clontarf Road
Dublin D03 PO46, Ireland
www.theliffeypress.com

A catalogue record of this book is
available from the British Library.

ISBN 978-1-7397892-5-1

Front cover image: *The Birth of the World* by Joan Miró (1925)
© Successió Miró / IVARO Dublin 2022

Printed in Bulgaria by Pulsio Print

Contents

Dedication

To Lesley, David and Fran
Always there and much loved

And to the memories of
Brid Ann Ryan and J. Kieran Taaffe
Friends for life – gone but not forgotten

When the striving stops,
the truth comes as a gift.

– Saul Bellow

Preface

Late in life, I was surprised to find a certain type of writing enjoyable. It drew me in, engaged me, passed the time, and helped with understanding some things in retrospect. I had little interest in writing an autobiography, or a structured memoir. They tell the story of a life or specific areas/events within it, and the material I had accumulated did not fit either category well. Would it make an interesting book? Perhaps, but I could not think of a way to pull it together. For example, a book of essays wouldn't work. Eventually, like all the best things, a title came unbidden, and fitted the material perfectly. And thus, *Tales from the Ivory Tower* was born.

Tales are more than an unembellished account of events. We have fairy tales, moral tales, mischievous tales and tall tales. And, of course, dead men tell no tales. A tale is longer than an anecdote and has something in common with a short story. It is imaginative, and can sometimes be intentionally untrue. Winston Churchill allegedly preferred a *Tale* to factual reports.

Here we must disappoint Churchill and, to borrow from Alan Bennett, these *Tales* are *mostly true* or *almost true*. Most started as relatively short pieces, accounts of events, places or people that moved, amused, or otherwise impressed and that fitted well together. They were often, revised, and bolted together during solitary time spent in Las Palmas in the Canaries. Time flew while I wrote or worked on them. Once started, it was seldom difficult to keep going. They created an energy of their own and made the mornings fly. They also include pieces that started as assignments in an MA course taken after retirement, or from homework for the Trinity Retirement Association writing group, or occasional extra-curricular creative writing sessions. These exercises helped break the rigid mould of scientific writing that imprisons and desiccates many accounts of a life in science.

The Ivory Tower suggests universities that are detached from society – places with an idyllic lifestyle. It can imply an appetite for ridiculous disputes like the medieval preoccupation with the number of angels that can be accommodated on the head of a pin. So, the Ivory Tower, and by implication the universities, are seen as impractical, sheltered, aloof, and esoteric. It is an elaborate metaphor for a state of mind.

The notion of Ivory Tower was around long before universities. It is taken from the Biblical Song of Songs, and suggested a person of great beauty, purity, and inaccessibility. Much later Pope Sixtus V, in 1587, approved its use among the glowing adjectives describing the Virgin Mary in the Litany dedicated to her. This became part of the routine household prayers in many parts of the world, lasting well into the twentieth century. It is a group prayer with a mantra-like content, taking about five minutes. The leader recites the titles and everybody else responds *Pray for us.* Here are a half dozen titles from the Litany:

Virgin most faithful,	*Pray for us.*
Seat of wisdom,	*Pray for us.*

Vessel of honour,	*Pray for us.*
Mystical rose,	*Pray for us.*
Tower of ivory,	*Pray for us.*
House of gold,	*Pray for us.*

I remember these clearly as part of evening family prayers up to the 1960s. They had a hypnotic impact and created a lifelong appreciation of the luminous quality that can attach to repetitive language. Later, when mantras arrived from the east, we already knew what they were.

Modern usage of the term Ivory Tower is detached from its religious/poetic roots. But it is relatively easy to make the connection via the image of a dreamer absorbed in a sense of mystery. This gained ground in the early to mid-twentieth century, possibly influenced by the skyline of Oxbridge university towns. During this period, it also gradually acquired negative overtones, suggesting that the detachment was not a caring one.

Nevertheless, universities are places of learning, escapist or otherwise. From time to time, specialist learning becomes critical to specific sectors. At that point, the sector impacted appreciates what the Ivory Tower can bring to its problems. This occurred during the Covid pandemic, when the Ivory Tower provided advice, assurance, vaccines and much more that helped humanity through a gargantuan crisis. This happens all the time in smaller ways, often barely noticed, when a niche problem in science, medicine, business and so on finds unlikley and able allies in the Ivory Tower. This is as it should be in a knowledge society, and sometimes enters the public domain in unexpected ways. The migration of the Ivory Tower into the names of our hospitals is an example. Take Cork University Hospital or St James's University Hospital, to name but two. Adding University to the names of hospitals is unlikely to be because it suggests that they are places of idle curiosity. Much more likely, it is to conjoin them with cutting edge knowledge that can enhance patient services.

The Ivory Tower to which I had the privilege of belonging, Trinity College Dublin, is often thought of as an oasis in the centre of the city. And, at least sometimes, it is just that. But it is also among the top tourist attractions in the state, something that intrudes on the presumed peace and seclusion within its walls. And yet there are nooks, and times when it magically reverts. On the other hand, many academics fully committed to the Ivory Tower energetically venture into the wider world and participate in its concerns. They bring new inspiration and perspectives, and are prolific contributors to the wider community, its cultural life, its businesses, its schools, its hospitals, its furious debates, its high-tech developments and its profoundly local social projects. Zest is added to life in a way that will never be quantified but should nonetheless be celebrated. The eccentric choice of topics in this book illustrates this universality of the university. Many of the activities mentioned were quietly facilitated by the Trustees of the Robert Boyle Foundation. They fostered work across science, religion, medicine, spirituality and the arts as though the hard borders, often present between these areas, were invisible.

So, what are the *Tales* about? The selection criteria, if such existed, had little to do with their importance – they are entirely predicated on how well and how fondly I remember the incident or event; whether I tended to tell stories about it; and/ or if it amused. Colleagues would make a different selection in a professional context. I didn't have to try to write about the topics here – they usually presented themselves unbidden and wanted to be written about. They are the memories from a life of scholarship and service that remain vivid, as opposed to things that are often, and legitimately, more highly rated. Others will have their own tales. A discerning eye will detect traces of the Ivory Tower in many streams of life. And finally, they include something not normally aspired to in universities or hospitals: an admittedly unsuccessful quest for wisdom as well as knowledge.

And what are the *Tales* not about? First and foremost, they are not intimate accounts of family or professional life. In my extended family, privacy and boundaries are well respected, and for the moment that excludes anything more than passing reference to its internal dynamics or the lives of those who are still with us. However, Chapter Six provides some insight into the generations that have passed. Time and distance may allow more freedom in this area.

Medical Physics, my profession, and its internal dynamic are, in the main, also excluded. Thus, current and former colleagues can rest easy. Almost all are excluded, with a few exceptions where a happy story with moral force requires that they be mentioned, usually with permission. For example, this is the case with Pat Plunkett in Chapter Ten. Sometimes, names are changed to protect the guilty (as well as the innocent). Where this is the case, the fictitious 'name' is presented in quotation marks when it first appears. But, professional life is a rich source and would be worth mining when those involved are no longer centre stage in their respective dramas.

Career successes and failures that seem overwhelmingly important at the time are by and large not very interesting when viewed from a distance. Securing major funding for a project, or approval for new staff or buildings, and even most career promotions don't leave an enduring impact. Occasionally they do, but in a minority of cases. For example, getting a new building put up and moving into it. After a few years most of the related excitement dims, and I seldom tell stories about what happened, even though at the time it was all consuming. What I remember are the small incidents that lend colour to the big projects. Unfortunately, within such projects, people don't have the room to be as colourful as they might otherwise be. And within a decade of its being completed, most of the people working in a large new building or institution will have little, if any, appreciation of what went into its creation.

Conversations are my best attempt to reconstruct them, often at considerable distance. Where it might be critical to a person's reputation, those involved were consulted, but normally I relied on memory. For convenience of narrative, conversations and characters are occasionally elided, or events are moved to another location. For example, the event involving Edna O'Brien at a Merriman Summer School (Chapter Three) occurred in Falls Hotel, Ennistymon, not as described in Lisdoonvarna.

The book consists of eleven chapters which are relatively independent of each other and can be read in any order. The chapters are grouped under four headings, *Arrived, Growth, Interlude,* and *Extra Curricular. Arrived,* in one chapter, deals with the almost surreal impact of Dublin traffic on work in the appointment I held in Trinity College prior to retirement.

The four chapters in *Growth* deal with early life, and life as a slow learning adult, trying to establish a sense of direction in the adult world. Chapter Two starts with a glimpse of the world of a young boy captivated by the ethereal beauty of the Bishop's high Mass in 1950s Ennis Cathedral. It led to a fascination with liturgy, clerical magic and later with foibles, not necessarily in the Father Ted league, but none the less amusing. It also eventually led to some wonderful years in Franciscan life. Much later the Merriman Summer School (Chapter Three) supported learning opportunities that would do credit to any university. It partnered this with an atmosphere of diversion, devilment, music, dance, and late-night conversations. Chapter Four deals with learning how to help people who turn to the Ivory Tower when things go astray and Chapter Five looks, in a very practical way, at what is shared by a life in science (physics) and the mystical/sense of awe that often is part of the spiritual life of individuals.

Interlude, the next two chapters, provides background about my parents and grandparents (Chapter Six) and, among other things, to important life skills picked up in school and refined in adult life, such as mitching from school/work and various forms of meditation (Chapter Seven).

The four chapters in *Extra Curricular* include risky travel to exotic places (Kuwait and Yemen) as part of academic life (Chapter Eight). Great art can influence and validate one's life as well as symbolically underwrite the work of large institutions like a university or the United Nations (Chapter Nine). People seek help from the Ivory Tower with the most unlikely problems (Chapter Ten). They range from trying to find a way around the points system for a talented student from an underprivileged background to an unexpected dying request entangled with drugs, death and a possibly troubled bishop on another continent. Or finding a solution to a thorny problem involving demolition of a chapel and its replacement in the sensitive world of the new National Children's Hospital. On a lighter note, Chapter Eleven is a celebration of the set dancing movement in Ireland, an activity that would have been worthy of a special place in the Ivory Tower, but through neglect didn't quite make it. It was an important part of Irish culture as it moved from the closed world of the mid-twentieth century to the *anything goes* approach of the last decades.

In summary, the *Tales* are an oblique look at one life spent in Trinity College, St James's Hospital and the international arena. They inevitably also provide a sideways glimpse into the inner workings of hospitals and universities. But more important, they are rooted in Dublin city and West Clare, were facilitated by the Robert Boyle Foundation, and are alert to the humour and wisdom encountered away from the vagaries of life inside the Ivory Tower. Their audience will hopefully include those whose lives are closely impacted by all the Ivory Towers we have created, and/or the healthcare system and, of course, the plain people of Ireland. The tales are sometimes sad, often happy, sometimes humorous, sometimes earnest, mostly true, and often elegiac for things Ireland needs but may not quite deserve.

Jim Malone
4 October 2022
Dublin

Arrived?

Chapter One

Getting There on the Bus ...!

... bloody buses –
You wait for about a year
And as soon as one approaches your stop
Two or three others appear.

– Wendy Cope, *Serious Concerns*

Traditionally, handover for new officeholders in Trinity College Dublin occurs in the high summer, specifically on twelfth of July, a date in the Irish calendar with troubled resonances. However, I had a good relationship with my predecessor, and while driving in that morning, reflected on how good tempered the change of Deans had been. I drove past the security man on the Lincoln Gate, almost expecting special recognition which, no surprise, was not forthcoming.

Passing playing fields and the physics and physiology departments, the faculty office came into view. Three things were special about the approach that morning. First, I had my own set of keys. Second, there was a reserved parking place for the Dean – something I had previously regarded with a feeling bordering on envy. Finally, and perhaps most important, a key to the private toilet – a place of solace and comfort for a man of advancing years whose prostate was beginning to assert its presence and, double jeopardy, whose physician had the bad manners to prescribe a diuretic.

The campus was quiet, and few cars were about. Everything looked well in the sun. College Park was green, not yet exhausted by the excesses of July and August. Few staff and even fewer students were in evidence. During term, at this time of day, it would have the frantic appeal of a disturbed anthill, with students rushing to and fro, parading from one lecture theatre to another. But that morning it was tranquil, and I relished it, not least for the privilege of parking without having to find a place. And even this was enhanced by the absence of cars in adjacent spaces, excellent for a person who liked to park in remote parts of County Clare.

∞   ∞   ∞

After three months, in early October, I thought the college was still enchanting, but different. Walking to the Westland Row end, after a meeting in the front square area, it bustled everywhere. Staff had re-emerged from their lairs after their summer 'hibernation'; students were energised by a new term and a new intake of freshers. The summer rush of tourists was not yet over, and enthusiastic crowds queued every day to see the Long Room, the Book of Kells, and the interpretative displays which were created a decade earlier for the Dublin city millennium.

I enjoyed the energy of their presence, especially the enthusiasm of the tourists and the advocates for the student societies, ranging from sedate choristers to the belligerent feminists. It was fresher's week; the societies laid out their sometimes eccentric stalls and pitched enthusiastically for new recruits. But I had been in the college long enough to feel a glimmer of jealousy about their enthusiasms and returning from a difficult meeting had more than a little cause to wonder at how they found the place so attractive. This ambivalence continued until after retirement, when an uncomplicated appreciation of the college and its charms, especially in the summer, returned.

But, to return to the downside, the reserved parking space so enjoyed a few months before was full on arrival that morning. I fumed and considered actions that might be appropriate, like letting down the miscreant's tyres or blocking them into the reserved parking place. But this would end in more trouble and more delay. So, it was back to seeking a space in obscure unfrequented corners. I fumed again, sought and eventually found an out-of-the-way spot.

This quickly became a pattern. According to parking cognoscenti, the only option was to arrive early and leave the car in position all day or find parking off site. The former was not practical for a faculty which had students, staff, researchers, laboratories, teaching facilities and buildings throughout the city and beyond, in teaching hospitals such St James's and Tallaght as well as a host of specialist hospitals and health agencies as far away as Wexford and Tullamore. The working day often started in one or other of the hospitals, moved to college and returned to the hospital, often doing the return journey more than once.

In addition, the Celtic tiger was beginning to roar, traffic in the city was congealing, and parking spaces were disappearing or had already vanished. A 1998/1999 interview on *Morning Ireland*, the main radio news programme on RTÉ, brilliantly illustrated the problem and went something like this:

David Hanley, the interviewer opened: 'We now turn to "Frank McMahon", who has first-hand experience of the parking difficulties in central Dublin. Good morning Frank. Tell us about yourself.'

Frank McMahon replied: 'Good morning, David. Thanks for the opportunity to talk about this. I work in Financial Services in the old docks area. We are a newly established international bank with a large turnover, and now have dozens of employees. We had planned to expand this to hundreds soon, but now I wonder if it is feasible.'

'Yes,' David said, 'there seems to be an enormous amount of development in the IFSC now, new banks and trading houses opening regularly?'

'You're right, there is new development all the time, lots of attractive new office buildings and state-of-the-art apartments. Also, a good range of shops and restaurants. And the old CHQ building is thriving, with up-market shops worthy of the financial community. But little or no parking has been provided with these developments. There is no public transport and it will be years before the promised Luas tram system comes on line.'

Frank paused and David asked, 'How do you manage now?'

'The short answer is we don't, and we don't see a break. We are completely boxed in, and it's not just the cost of housing. Gridlock and lack of parking are hampering our plans.'

'What do you do yourself?'

'Out of sheer exasperation,' Frank replied, 'I just bought an apartment in a new stylish block on the river, not far from O'Connell Bridge. It set me back nearly a quarter of a million and has a parking place to go with it.'

'And are you looking forward to apartment living right in the centre of the city? Do you have a young family and children?'

'The answer is no and no. I live in Howth and have no intention of living cooped up in a city centre apartment. I bought it only for the convenience of the parking place!'

And David Hanley brought the interview to a close. 'Thank you, Frank McMahon. Happy parking there, in what must be the most expensive parking place in the world. Now we go to a break.'

And so, in the centre of the city at that time, it became impossible to get parking. I remember this interview as I lived in the same block and had a parking space there. Later I also established that the apartment in question was a vacant near mine. However, there was no question of taking the car out to drive to another part of the city during the working day. So, the car stayed in it, often parked for weeks on end. This had multiple consequences, some of which are encountered in what follows.

∞   ∞   ∞

After an exhausting analysis, it was clear that a change in tack was required and, thus, I reluctantly became a regular client of Dublin Bus. I gradually relearned the city bus system, becoming a bus-bore and expert on the routes and schedules. An early favourite was the 123 bus from Marino, through the city centre, through the grounds of St James's Hospital and on to Drimnagh. It was then a small, red and yellow, nipper-style single decker, about one-third the length of an ordinary bus.

The 123 quickly attracted a strangely eclectic group of people. Of course, there were locals, but there were also many students from the nursing, medical and allied professions. In the early days a small number of adventurous consultants signed up, but they generally tried to travel incognito, and did not join in the colourful conversations that often shortened journeys.

'How 'ya, Gemma. Is your fella still in jail?'

'Yea. He'll be there till next year. But it gives me a bit a peace.'

'Mine too. But he'll be out soon. Don't know where we'll get the money to look after him. Goin' to see him in Clover Hill today, and the bollix'll start a fight. Where are you goin'?'

'To court – for robbin'. But, I don't do robbin' people any-more, only rob shops now. Them guards has me knackered. Why don't they leave ya alone when you're botherin' nobody?'

Unrepeatable conversations from that era still lodge in the memory. There were also some decidedly colourful and dodgy characters.

After a bruising and exhausting morning meeting in college, I vividly recall getting on the 123 on Dame Street to head back to St James's to deal with an equally obnoxious and long-forgotten issue. For the first time, a kind, middle-aged lady offered me her seat. Shamefully, I gratefully accepted but can only imagine the ashen spectacle that must have presented itself to her. She must have presumed she was dealing with a seriously ill old man heading for resuscitation in the hospital.

I became habituated to the bus and, eventually, was able to read and absorb the papers for meetings on the trip to or from college. The proposal for the degree course in nursing was active at the time. It was contentious and resulted in some heated meetings. At one stage the proposal was referred for a major overhaul. The revised proposal was circulated for discussion at a high-level, large college meeting, and I was detailed to introduce it.

It was a substantial document. I was studying it carefully on the 123 on the way to college for the meeting. A well-preserved, middle-aged woman seated beside me was also reading it over my shoulder, obviously with great interest. But she was slower than me, and irritated when I began to tidy the papers and proposal into my bag as we moved down Dame Street. She caught my eye and held it.

'Rubbish,' she said, 'absolute rubbish! It won't make one bit of difference. It won't improve nurses or nursing.'

I excused myself and left the bus in haste. Unfortunately, the message she left ringing in my ears accurately foretold the reception the proposal was about to receive in formal session in college. For the record, the meeting was hostile, contentious and, at one stage, as close to becoming a riot as I had experienced. However, after a few more twists and turns, it survived and undergraduate degrees in nursing and in midwifery were duly introduced. My fellow traveller on the 123 would, no doubt, be unimpressed.

Travel by public transport also offered many interesting off-bus moments. A bus in an unusual environment can create an unexpected ambience at variance with its normal purpose and image. This occurred when the 123 first started to travel through the grounds of St James's Hospital. The bus created an atmosphere of municipal connectedness that, up until then, had been missing. It emphasised an aura, an atmosphere, a level of engagement with the city and the local community. Something like this had been targeted by the hospital, but it escaped visibility until the bus started to pass back and forth through the grounds. Somehow, the hospital was no longer an Ivory Tower distanced from its community;

it now welcomed the citizens it served on their own terms in a relaxed way. For some time, I had entertained these thoughts, but felt they were probably just part of a private fantasy world, until the day the 123 bus appeared prominently on the cover of the hospital's annual report.

The ultimate off-bus experience arrived when the new Luas Red Line opened. In a way, it might be regarded as a virtual Trinity Medical School project in that it directly connected the college in the centre of town with its two main teaching hospitals, St James's and Tallaght. It passed directly through the St James's campus, with a stop, James's, just inside the main gate and right beside the School of Medicine buildings at one end. At the other, the Fatima stop is just outside the hospital boundary and initially seemed remote. But the big new children's hospital took advantage of vacant office space right beside it and, with great foresight, located its planning and building offices there, which created a silent shift in the centre of gravity for the campus. Thus, the Red Line has, perhaps inadvertently, enhanced the sense of the hospital campus being intimately connected to the city. It is surprising that this is seldom, if ever, mentioned by those debating the accessibility of the location.

After St James's, the Luas continues its long, winding journey to Tallaght, where the other main teaching hospital for the college is situated. Tallaght Hospital is a long linear building, possibly as long as Grafton Street. Unfortunately, neither of the two Luas stops for Tallaght Hospital is well located with respect to accessing the main patient entrance. This is surprising, as much of the building work on the Luas line and the hospital occurred around the same time.

The Red Line also has some relatively colourful characters among its clientele at the Abbey and Jervis city centre stops, where drug pushers and their customers are evident. The courts address the problems of various participants in this trade at the Four Courts, Smithfield and Heuston stops, while the addicts are treated at James's. But the city centre stops dramatically emphasise the connectedness of this troubled aspect of city life: addiction, the drug trade, crime, punishment and destruction of the health of a young population. Regardless of these reminders, the Luas is a great success and has normalised the use of public transport among the medical school staff and students, as well as patients and doctors in the hospitals.

On a different note, an opportunity was missed in not allowing the Red Line to go under, over or through Trinity College. This would have avoided diverting the tracks onto the heavily congested vehicle and pedestrian traffic of College Green and O'Connell Street. The expense and delay of going under the college might have been considerable, but is unlikely to exceed the expense and inconvenience to all the city traffic now discommoded by the Luas having to pass through College Green. Passing through the college and up Marlborough Street would also have rehabilitated the street and removed some pressure from O'Connell Street. A bold vision would have served the city better and the college might have gained a municipal ally as did St James's Hospital.

Meanwhile, in the days before the Luas, when you were unlucky and missed the 123 within the hospital, a short walk brought you to a bus stop just outside the main entrance. The buses from this stop were double-deckers which, from upstairs, provided great views of city life. One of the most striking was the frequent funerals from St James's Church near the Guinness Brewery. What distinguished these was the uncharacteristically large proportion of young people attending. I surmised, though never verified, that the deceased were often young addicts being mourned by their peers. A potent reminder of the devastation of young lives in an underprivileged inner city area.

Many interesting conversations occurred while waiting at the bus stop outside the hospital, including occasionally being offered lifts to town – not always welcome. The price of accepting a lift could involve an intense bout of lobbying on some hospital or university issue. A memorable encounter occurred one day while I was standing at the stop, musing on the many things that one muses on at bus stops, including the weather, or how to outwit an opponent in one of the day's encounters, or what one might have for lunch. I was distracted from this pleasant reverie by a large car emerging aggressively, at speed, from the hospital, and turning right as it accelerated toward the city centre. Passing the bus stop, it suddenly braked, screeched to a halt some distance down the road, and rapidly reversed to the bus stop. The front passenger door opened and the driver invited me to *sit in*.

The driver was a formidable academic consultant and a member of a large north Dublin family of doctors. A gastroenterologist with boundless energy, he had an unparalleled commitment to developing services for his patients. He was an acknowledged expert on endoscopy and manoeuvred endoscopes, upper or lower, into places that others failed to reach. There was a rumour that if one saw a one-euro coin on the floor of his department, bending down to pick it up was to invite a colonoscopy. Here we give him the pseudonym 'Dr Nelson Salmon'.

I knew Nelson well and was delighted to receive his characteristically dramatic offer of a lift, and bundled myself, with a large briefcase and a tatty coat, into his pristine car. He was immaculately suited and scented. In his company, I felt like a vagrant. He looked at me, conveying a sense that I should know better about something.

'Good morning, Dean,' he intoned.

'And good morning to you, Sir,' I replied. 'How many lives have you saved today, Doctor?'

'Oh!' he replied with a fall in his voice. 'My efforts have been totally obstructed, with our chairman *the worm doctor* leading the pack. I spent the morning apologising to patients whose endoscopies and colonoscopies were cancelled as the day beds were filled with the overnight take from the emergency department. So, I've nothing to do, zero, nada – and you're the beneficiary.'

The *worm doctor*, a distinguished Trinity zoologist, had been appointed chairman of the hospital board by the Minister for Health. He oversaw a policy whereby patients arriving at the emergency department would be admitted to whatever beds were available, including day beds for procedures like endoscopy. Nelson continued: 'But I told each patient how to find the *worm doctor's* office, and what they should say to him when they got there.'

A conversation on this emerging and later familiar crisis followed, but he quickly tired of it.

'But listen,' he said. 'That's not the reason I picked you up.'

'Oh!'

'It's not good enough, and you must stop,' he continued.

I was puzzled, feeling he had abandoned the beds crisis topic, and replied: 'But the chairman is doing all he can. What else do you think he might do?'

21

'No,' he replied, 'that's not what I'm talking about. What I mean is, it's not good enough for our Dean to be standing at the bus stop outside the hospital. What would consultants from other hospitals think?'

'Well,' I said, 'I suspect doctors from other hospitals don't care much. They have enough problems of their own.'

He paused and retorted: 'You must stop this. It would look bad to private patients and wouldn't help development of the private hospital.'

And there it was; and perhaps he was right. Another revelation among the many that result from using public transport. The banter continued, but he had made his point. We were approaching the city centre, and when the time came, he dropped me off with courtesy and something approximating charm. I then went to a long-forgotten college meeting, and suspect he had the rest of the day off. I continued to frequent the bus stop outside the hospital. Interestingly, though, I didn't forget Nelson's advice, but did nothing about it.

Over the years, I got many lifts from St James's bus stops. Nelson's dramatic screeching to a halt was near the beginning of my period in office. Toward the end, I had an encounter that, perhaps, illustrates what happens when power and influence are slipping away. Instead of a large car screeching past, this event started much more mildly. Tony Bates, a well-known psychologist with a column in *The Irish Times* and regular radio appearances, emerged from the hospital on an old-fashioned bicycle, turned right and headed toward town. He passed the bus stop without recognition, even though we worked closely together on a cognitive psychotherapy programme he ran. However, once past the stop, he wobbled in delayed recognition and wobbled again wondering should he stop. The latter prevailed and he pulled over about 50 metres down the road. I walked toward him. On drawing level, we exchanged greetings and small talk and then he said:

'There are rumours you're stepping down from the deanship and retiring. Are they true?'

'Yes!' I replied, perhaps a little concerned that I might be about to appear as an anecdote in *The Irish Times*.

'Would you consider staying on a bit longer? There's still lots to be done.'

'Well,' I said, anxious to frame a psychologically plausible response. 'When I started this job, I promised I'd stay for as long as it was enjoyable. And while that was the case for a long time, recent months have been very difficult, and the bad days outnumber the good by a clear margin.'

'Still,' he replied, 'there is a lot to be done in areas you are committed to. Don't be hasty.'

I paused and considered, and then said something that hadn't even entered my mind prior to his pressing the issue. 'But, there are so many things I want to do. If I don't give this job up, there will be no room to grow into them and they'll never be done –!'

We reverted to small talk, and soon we went on our respective ways. In a perverse way the psychologist won. I vividly remember this exchange and suspect that it was framed to impress him.

Much of the above happened long ago around the turn of the new millennium, when the Celtic tiger was getting into its stride and at the same time a lesser recession, known as the dot.com bubble, was threatening. House prices were beginning to be a problem, and college recruitment to senior positions was adversely affected. I recall several searches for new professors that went the course, with the appointment being offered, the candidate being genuinely interested, and the process then unravelling when the impossibility of buying a house in a good suburb on a professor's salary became clear. This was exacerbated as time went by, and we spent a decade selling and buying houses to each other, driving prices up further, and we all know where that ended.

Traffic and parking problems continued to be difficult, and by the time of my retirement in 2002 I was considering abandoning being a motorist altogether. But this was a gradual affair, more a case of drifting into it, responding to events and movements that demanded attention. These included the increasing impracticality of being able to use a car effectively for its intended purpose while living in the city centre. This meant long periods during which I didn't use the car; it sat immobile in its expensive parking space.

Occasionally, when I went to get the car, it wasn't in the apartment carpark, where it should be. The most common explanation was that sometime earlier I had taken it to visit a family member. After the visit, I absentmindedly returned to town on the bus, and left the car somewhere in the vicinity of the visit. A week or two later, this sequence of events generally emerged from memory, and the car was relocated sitting unattended outside the house of the friend or relation in question. Shades of the absent-minded professor.

The most dramatic in this series of mishaps occurred several weeks after attending a conference in London. For one reason or another, I needed the car and went to the carpark – it wasn't there. I retraced possible occasions when it might have been inadvertently left in the suburbs or institutional carparks in town, all to no avail. And then the London conference occurred to me: had I used the car to get to the airport? No, at that time I had ceased driving to the airport and always used public transport to get there and back. I checked and double-checked my memory but had no recollection of driving to the airport. A dead end, and for a while I began to wonder if it had been stolen.

Gradually, the veil lifted, and out of the mists the experience of taking a flight from Shannon Airport to get to London emerged. This happened because I spent a weekend in Clare in connection with the Merriman Summer School. The opportunity to travel directly from Shannon to London presented itself as the solution to a time management problem. Parking at Shannon, at that time, was not a problem and not expensive, although a prominent sign outside the main terminal warned: 'Don't even think about parking here'. So I found a free day, took the train to Limerick, got the bus onwards to Shannon Airport and there in the carpark, not too far from the terminal, sat my neglected car.

That was a defining moment in becoming a non-motorist. I used the car so little that over a month had passed and, not alone had I not noticed its absence but had no recollection of where it was. It was a significant step beyond not being able to find it in the carpark. However, it took a little longer for the final parting with the car to occur. Again, this was unplanned, and arose when my daughter's car was damaged beyond repair, and I offered her the use of mine while she considered what to do. I gave the car a wistful glance as she drove away and it disappeared around the corner, knowing that this was not a short-term loan and my days as a motorist had come to an end.

As a footnote, the most valuable aspect of that car may have been an approximately 7 centimetre square piece of paper affixed to the windscreen. No, not the tax disc. Rather, a valid parking permit for Trinity College, which at the weekend still had free spaces. An enterprising person coming of age around then would value this as a classy accessory.

∞   ∞   ∞

Thereafter, I stopped being a motorist for well over a decade and have no recollection of missing a car. However new skills had to be acquired, and I learned about the bus routes, and acquired the apps for Dublin Bus, Luas, DART, trains etc. and became proficient in their use. As time passed, I was genuinely surprised at the generosity of motorists in offering lifts to places throughout the country that beckoned for professional and/or leisure reasons, including West Clare for the Merriman Summer School and Lismore for the Boyle Summer School, as well as Limerick, Tullamore, Mullingar, Glendalough, Waterford, Cork, Croome, Tubbercurry, Sligo, Longford, Nenagh, Milltown Malbay, Ennistymon, Adare, Killaloe, Ennis, Tulla, Galway, Spiddal, Dundalk and Rostrevor, for reasons too numerous to mention, but all locations difficult to access with public transport. I am grateful to all the generous drivers in whose passenger seats I have been privileged to travel.

The happy state of being a non-motorist eventually came to an end more than a decade later and arose from chronic foot problems that threatened mobility. As a result, in 2014 I decided to purchase a car again, but on this occasion opted for one of the then relatively new electric vehicles. And, having lost the skill of motorway driving, I decided to confine motoring to the city. This has been a great success:

the car has minimal environmental impact on the noise and fuel-polluted city streets, and it is a pleasure to drive. Rather than agitating, it creates a sense of calm, with no noise and very little burden on the diminishing head space available as one ages. At the time of writing, I am on my third electric car, which I use minimally, about a tenth of an average motorist's use, and have found a way of life that is not disrupted by unavailable parking. I still enjoy public transport and the services, for over a decade, of an almost saintly taxi driver (but that's another tale).

GROWTH

Chapter Two

Barchester Moments: Clerics, Fascinating Failings and Foibles

Two things fill the mind with ever new and increasing wonder and awe…: the starry heavens above and the moral law within.

– Immanuel Kant's tombstone

*T*he *Barchester Chronicles* are part of the enduring legacy of nineteenth century English novelist, Anthony Trollope. He charted the cut and thrust of clerical life in a fictional English county and its cathedral town of Barchester. Much later, a distant descendent, Joanna Trollope, did the same for a twentieth century Anglican Rector and his wife. Almost unknown among these giants of popular literature are the wonderful clerical novels of Canon Sheehan (1852-1913) of Doneraile, County Cork. He created a sympathetic and, by today's standards, innocent account of clerical life in Ireland. I read most of them as a youth; they influenced me, and I found much worthy of emulation in them. In addition, I have often been fascinated by clerical foibles, not quite in the *Father Ted* mould, but nonetheless memorable, moving and amusing.

∞　　∞　　∞

From age five to ten I lived about halfway between the Clare county town of Ennis and a small village directly south of it. On shopping trips we passed the cathedral of Saints Peter and Paul, our parish church, seat of the Catholic bishops of Killaloe, across the street from the Old Ground Hotel. My father and one of my brothers attended Sunday mass there every week, while my mother stayed at home to look after a growing brood of smaller children. Mass in Latin on these occasions was accompanied by choral singing, plain or Gregorian Chant, lots of incense, and the mitred, elaborately vested bishop. It was a more lavish and moving ceremony than that normally experienced in a provincial church and, for me, started a lifelong love of ritual, and became the benchmark for how liturgy should be. Even a seven-year-old could relate to its combination of a reflective mood and beauty.

My memory of Archbishop Michael Fogarty is of a small, dignified man. It was hard to imagine how anybody in the town could be more important than him. Later, I learned that he had been a key figure during the formative years of the new state, lending valuable support to Eamon de Valera. This added depth to his character but, to my young mind, it diminished him. It reduced him from the direct connection with the sacred (whatever that means) and the beauty of what happened in the cathedral, to somebody who did ordinary important things and was well regarded for them. I didn't understand why people were impressed (or angered) by his contributions to the state and politics. What he did in the cathedral was so overwhelmingly more moving than anything else I encountered in a world that was monochrome, pre-TV, DVD and even vinyl records.

Archbishop Fogarty was about 90 years of age at this time, the early to mid-1950s. He had been a bishop for the best part of 50 years, which may account for his fluency and ease with liturgy. In my memory, his ceremonies win hands down, when compared with even the best of academic ceremonies (for example, graduations). But all good things come to an end, and a coadjutor bishop, Joseph Rogers, was appointed with rights of succession, and began to replace him regularly on Sundays. He was a more energetic, grounded figure, and while the liturgies still had something of a magical quality, a level of realism began to intrude.

This was because of Bishop Rogers's sermons. He almost always referred to the English Sunday newspapers, which he condemned roundly for reasons a small boy could not understand. It is possible that his reasons were not simple or pure. For example, his intention might have been to support the *Sunday Press*, de Valera's own newspaper, which owed much to Bishop Fogarty. However, even a young mind could detect that the criticism also related to something unsavoury. This applied with even greater force to the *Sunday People*, often singled out for special attention. Much later, I came to realise the unsavoury matters were sex scandals.

Something of Archbishop Fogarty's more nuanced approach to events can be gleaned from the following exchange with Andy McEvoy, sometime editor of the *Clare Champion* and the *Limerick Leader*.

'Why don't you go to mass, Andy?' the bishop asked.

'I am not allowed to,' the editor replied. 'I was excommunicated a lifetime ago by Bishop O'Dwyer.'

'Yerrah, Andy, forget about it,' said the bishop. 'Shure O'Dwyer was mad; everyone knew that. Will I see you at my mass on Sunday?'

Andy McEvoy's son was present on this occasion, reported the conversation, and tells us his father was occasionally seen in the cathedral after that and remained friendly with the bishop. But his father's Saturday night reading continued to be booklets from the Rationalist Press Association, even more challenging than the English Sunday newspapers.

∞   ∞   ∞

I find it strange that memory of the cathedral liturgies is so vivid, when I have no memory of many other important religious occasions, for example, first communion. At age about ten we moved to Dublin, and I can recall confirmation in St Agatha's Church, just off the North Strand. The presiding prelate, the imperious Archbishop of Dublin, John Charles McQuaid, moved in elaborate, full pontifical robes through the class asking catechism questions of the candidates.

'What is the Blessed Trinity?' he reportedly asked one boy.

'I don't understand it,' the nervous boy stuttered.

'You're not meant to: it's a mystery!' the Archbishop responded and flounced on, robes trailing, to the next over-awed candidate. But, though commanding, the Archbishop of Dublin didn't rate in terms of liturgy and ceremony. An Archbishop Fogarty he wasn't.

Thereafter, liturgy lost something for me, sidelined by emerging adolescence and, in due course, by the pressures of academic and professional life. It was decades before it reasserted itself. In my mid-forties, with time on my hands on a Sunday afternoon in Paris, I chanced into Notre Dame cathedral. A service was in progress, and I sat quietly at the back of the central area reserved for participants. It was a benediction, and I was captivated and transported back to Ennis's cathedral. But the scale was grander: flowing vestments and a wonderful choir contributed, as did lighting, candles and generous quantities of incense that seemed to billow from two large open dishes over a metre in diameter and suspended at head height on each side of the high alter. At the time of writing, it is sad to recall that the world was deprived of this special place by the dreadful fire that destroyed it on the evening of 15 April 2019.

In the mid to late 1980s, I started to rediscover Clare and was lucky enough to chance on both the Willie Clancy and the Merriman Summer Schools (Chapter Three). The latter was so absorbing that I became a member of its organising committee, which on a sunny August evening in 2001 hosted a dinner attended by Bishop Willie Walsh, successor to Bishops Fogarty and Rogers. It is unlikely that this saintly man's sermons had much to say about the English Sunday newspapers. And it is highly likely that his appointment was a *clerical* error that slipped through the Vatican's bureaucracy. He was, in his characteristically gentle but firm way, seriously at odds with much that it held rigidly.

I visited the cathedral of Saints Peter and Paul again around 2012. Like many places enshrined in childhood memories, it seemed to have shrunk. It appeared small in scale, even beside the large, basilica-like parish churches of the inner Dublin suburbs, not to mention Notre Dame. But it was clear it was lovingly cared for and well maintained, and outside was something on the grand scale – a large sculpture of two caring, human hands, by Shane Gilmore. It is worthy of Willie Walsh, during whose tenure it was commissioned and installed in 2008.

Over the years, Bishop Roger's injunction about buying the English Sunday newspapers often came to mind, never more so than when leaving mass on a Sunday and seeing them piled high on the temporary stalls that appeared outside so many churches. *The People*, while it still existed, and the *News of the World* tended to have extra-large piles. How to square this with the view that the Catholic Church dominated the country makes a curious, if somewhat improbable, reflection. I suspect there is a good PhD in it for a social sciences student.

I encountered a variant on the theme of English Sunday newspapers while attending the Merriman Summer School sometime in the early 1990s. Paddy Hillery, who had been President of Ireland, was patron of the school. He maintained a house in his native place, just outside Milltown Malbay in West Clare. I had a house on the other side of the village, and on the Sunday morning in question dropped into Hurley's newsagent/confectioner/multifunction shop.

'A fine morning!' Mrs Hurley announced from behind the counter as I entered.

'Yes, indeed,' I replied, and without pause moved straight to my slightly guilty request: 'Do you have an *Observer*?' At the time, *The Observer* was a quality English Sunday broadsheet, some would say along the lines of *The Guardian*.

'Is it The *Observer* you want?' she replied, emphasising the definite article in a way that suggested there might be trouble in store – which instantly transported me back to the long-deceased Bishop Roger's sermons.

'Yes,' I replied bravely. She edged sideways, crablike, toward a connecting door to the kitchen at the back of the shop. She pushed the door open a little with her foot and shouted into the kitchen:

'Is Paddy Hillery down this weekend?'

'No,' came the disembodied reply.

'There you are now,' she said. 'The weather mustn't be good enough for him.' After a pause, she continued: 'You can have The *Observer* then,' again emphasising the definite article. 'There's not much call for it around here.'

And so, on that Sunday I became the unique possessor of the only copy of that English Sunday newspaper in Milltown Malbay and the surrounding area. From time to time since, I've amused myself trying to figure out how Paddy Hillery might have dealt with the situation decades earlier when, as a politician and government minister, he would have been aware of the injunctions from the bishop's seat in Ennis.

∞   ∞   ∞

In late September 1963, two years after the Leaving Certificate, I boarded a train in Dublin bound for Killarney. This followed a summer working in a hospital near Luton, where I read the English Sunday newspapers every week, and noted the absence of thunderbolts from the sky. My destination was Killarney's Franciscan friary, which housed the novitiate in which new candidates for the order spent their first year. It was an unsurprising destination given the earlier fascination with things liturgical. The first week or so is a blur of many new things. The group of about 25 that had joined were assigned modest individual rooms, and all the possessions we brought with us, including most of our clothing, was handed up (or, more accurately, taken away).

Our accommodation was on the top (second) floor and attic of the friary, which was a pleasant nineteenth century building. We were not allowed go to the other floors, except to the church and refectory. We could go into the large gardens with two to three metre high solid Victorian walls. The church was graced with an extraordinary gothic altar that many would now find to be over the top. The spacious sanctuary had more than enough choir stalls for the new novices and the community of resident friars. It was visually separated from the area of the church occupied by the congregation. There was no contact between the new novices and the congregation or anybody from outside the monastery. Within a week of joining, we were completely cut off from the outside world, including family, radio, TV, newspapers and much more.

The isolation continued for a full year, and I can only recall one occasion on which it was relaxed. This was when we were told of the assassination of President John F. Kennedy sometime after it happened. This was a jolt, a shock, to realise how we had become so distanced from events of real importance. It emphasised how far we had drifted from the concerns of everyday life in less than few short months. One of our number had been preparing a presentation drawing on Kennedy's speeches, with no knowledge that he had been shot. Had he not been working on this we might not have been told. With the benefit of hindsight, I am shocked not to have been disturbed by our level of isolation.

The room furnishings were simple: a metal-framed single bed, a chair, a table that served as a desk, a small cupboard and bookshelf, and a washstand with basin and large jug for water. I was lucky enough to have a room that looked out toward the mountains and cathedral church some distance away. The town's people and general activity in the nearby area could not be seen due to the high walls. I have vivid memories of cold, bright sunny mornings when clouds sat halfway up the large mountains with peaks emerging above them.

The clothing we were given consisted of old-fashioned shirts without a collar. The latter could be affixed with a device like a small version of a cufflink, referred to as a stud. The fabric was heavy and rough as they were made to last a lifetime. My maternal grandfather used to wear shirts like this, so I was familiar with them. In addition, ordinary trousers with the legs turned up or knee length shorts were worn. Over these the Franciscan habit was thrown, a long, loose, full-length dark brown tunic with wide sleeves and deep pockets under the arms. A double length of long white cord gathered this loose garment at the waist and the cord had three knots at one end representing the vows of religious life: poverty, chastity and obedience. The loose tunic was augmented with a hood that sat on the shoulders and could be pulled up over the head to stave off rain or cold. An outer cloak-like garment was available if one was going outside to the garden or if it was very cold in the house. And at night it was. We normally went to bed about 9.00 pm but were roused again at midnight several times a week to spend 40 minutes or so in the freezing church singing the morning portions of the divine office in Latin.

Shoes and socks were not worn. Instead, it was open sandals all year, regardless of weather, as required by the Franciscan rule, although those with health issues could get exemptions. My memory is that few, if any, in our group required such exemptions. In fact, it is well known that most heat is lost through the head, and traditional advice had it that 'the best way to keep your feet warm is to wear a hat'.

While a few of our group were less than congenial, for the most part the experience was positive and rewarding. Extensive exposure to liturgy, and the extra dimension of a reflective inner life largely driven by religious considerations, was both challenging and life changing. For some in the group, the experience of a previously unexplored inner life was disturbing, and for others it was exciting and had its ecstatic moments. This quasi-mystical and risky aspect of religious experience was quite at variance with a rigorous logical approach that had been inculcated in, for example, apologetics classes in secondary school (Chapters Five and Seven).

∞　　∞　　∞

The first year also introduced us to ancient patterns of life and prayer in the monastic traditions of the Christian churches. While love of liturgy grew with experience, so also did a more intellectually critical approach to the life. For example, I became acutely aware that when one entered the sanctuary, 'The Holy of Holies', what one found there was – in the empirical sense – nothing. No doubt some found this to be an offensive observation. However, it was accompanied by parallel insights, which in the fullness of time led me to a profound sense of the mystery at the heart of all experience, whether in personal life, science, the arts, theology or variants on the religious life in Christian and other cultures (Chapter Five). This matured over 50 years and found its way into a book written with a friend, John McEvoy, who shared these experiences of a half century ago. The book, *Mystery and the Culture of Science,* reflects on how hard borders between the sciences, the arts and religious studies impoverish all three.

The level of isolation relaxed at the end of the first year when we moved to Galway to attend the university. However, isolation from family and former friends continued. Mobile phones, social media, the internet and financially accessible travel were still many years away. Visits by family were limited to one or two per year at most, and we were not allowed to visit them at home. Almost forty years later, toward the end of her life, my mother told me that she felt this unyielding separation was deeply wrong, although she had not complained about it at the time, and seldom spoke ill of anybody or anything. Nevertheless, she was supportive of my joining, and made it clear that she would be equally supportive of my leaving. This was reassuring as something of failure was still associated with dropping out of religious life. The phrase 'spoiled priest' was still used for those in such situations, and nuns leaving convents was virtually unheard of, though it certainly happened.

∞   ∞   ∞

The life changing years that followed deserve more attention than is possible here. Enough for now to say they allowed personal growth and evolution of a rich worldview, arising from living closely with so many others studying the arts, languages, sociology, politics, philosophy, mathematics and the sciences.

In 1968, I parted company with the Franciscans and moved to Glasgow to undertake a PhD in Medical Physics and work in the health service (Chapter Five). There, Lesley Hooper and I met and later we were married, which introduced new dimensions of liturgy and Christian life. Lesley was from the Anglican tradition which, in Scotland, was the Episcopal Church. We both sometimes attended its cathedral church in Glasgow, a largely Presbyterian and frankly sectarian city.

However, we also often attended Sunday mass at the Catholic Chaplaincy of the University of Glasgow. Gerard Hughes, the chaplain, was an exceptional and inspirational figure to find in these surroundings. He was a breath of fresh air and experimented with liturgy in a quiet way. As a Jesuit, he had freedom to explore new approaches and was particularly influenced by a period of theological study in Germany after World War II. He was imbued with this and with the theology of Vatican II, which had just ended. Subsequently, he had more than his share of difficulties with the Archbishop of Glasgow, who dismissed, and sometime later reinstated, him. His difficulties with the Archbishop, and the church, related to his practice of inclusion of those from other churches during Sunday mass, and to Pope Paul VI's teaching on contraception (in *Humanae Vitae* just issued). Later, he went on to become a celebrated retreat master and writer on the spiritual life, and occasionally lived in Manresa, a Jesuit house, directly across the road from my family home in Clontarf in Dublin.

When it came to arranging a 'mixed marriage', I felt that Gerry Hughes was a person who could be trusted and might be able to help, so I made an appointment to meet him in the Chaplaincy early in 1970. He was helpful, and his counsel was wise, but promised difficulty. He was excluded from organising weddings and I would have to make the practical arrangements with a Father Cornelius O'Leary, Parish Priest of Hillhead, where we lived. I set up a meeting and on the appointed evening entered the hall of a poorly lit, dark parish house, with a pervasive smell of damp and cooking that owed more to the depressed 1930s than the 1970s.

I was shown into an equally dim reception room and awaited the Parish Priest. He was a thickset, elderly man, in a dark soutane whose appearance did nothing to lighten the gloom. I rose to greet him and shake hands. He ignored this and flopped heavily into an equally heavy chair at the corner of the table.

'So, you're the young buck who wants to marry a Protestant,' he barked in a rich Kerry accent, unaltered by a lifetime in Glasgow. I was taken aback, and though I had heard of clerical arrogance I had no experience of something like this. The stakes were high, and unsure of how to respond, mumbled something non-committal.

'Hmph,' he snorted. 'There won't be many rosaries in that house. Now, young man, you need my permission to go through with this, and to get it you will do as I tell you.'

He embarked on an explanation of the *Ne Temere* decree, which required the children of a mixed marriage to be brought up as Catholics. Furthermore, he made it clear that any 'nonsense' from the university or its chaplain would not be entertained. And so, one of the most unpleasant experiences of the Catholic Church I had to date began, and the rant continued as it started, belligerent and shocking. Much later, he began to draw the business to a close.

'Now,' he announced, 'come back here next week with that unfortunate girl you're about to marry and we'll see what to do.'

'Okay,' I responded, and departed shocked, confused and with no idea how this was going to turn out.

∞　∞　∞

A week later, I returned to the dark room with Lesley only partly prepared for an anticipated car crash. Somehow the room was a little brighter. Father O'Leary made a dramatic entrance, with a smile so large and gracious that it seemed to precede him. He directed his greeting exclusively to Lesley:

'You are so welcome my dear. Now let us see how we can help you!'

43

She was shocked, and although the account of the previous encounter she received was sanitised, this was not expected. I was completely thrown and had no idea how to respond to his new mood. The discussion went smoothly, he withheld consent but graciously explained the constraints he had to work with. She listened, and I was gobsmacked. Eventually, he agreed to provide the various letters of permission needed for the wedding to proceed in Birmingham, Lesley's home place. On our part, we accepted the *Ne Temere* terms, but there was something of de Valera's empty formula about it, and in less than an hour we emerged into the welcoming light of a dark street and heaved a sigh of relief.

The wedding liturgy was conducted in the surrounds of a beautiful church of modern design, St Catherine of Siena's, in central Birmingham, by a priest sympathetic to the situation and with the collaboration of the Anglican rector involved. Our children were dealt with on their own terms and have probably never heard of the *Ne Temere* decree.

And so back to a less fraught experience of church and churchmen.

∞   ∞   ∞

The first time I didn't meet the late Cardinal Daly was around 1966. Then, long before he became the head of the Irish Catholic Church, he was a priest in Belfast and I was a student studying physics in Galway. Though still in the Franciscans I was delegated to attend a physics students' conference at Queen's University in Belfast. It may seem strange that this travel was allowed while, at the same time, we were not permitted to visit our homes. But this was one of the many contradictions in how the world managed itself at that time. As with not being told about President Kennedy's demise,

I'm now shocked that it did not occur to me to question these strange boundaries until much later.

On this first occasion of not meeting the future cardinal, the order had arranged accommodation with a Franciscan philosopher, Theodore Crowley, who taught at Queen's. He lived on the ground floor of a large Victorian house and was a gracious, entertaining and memorable host for a young student. The upper story was a separate apartment occupied by another scholarly priest, Cahal Daly, who was also taught philosophy. I was in the house for several days, and could sense his comings and goings, but never met him. My host advised, in the most diplomatic way, that it was best not to intercept him as, he implied without saying so, he could be hard going. During the 50 years that followed, I had several near misses, not meeting him in ways that seemed curious. His memory remained vivid, as awareness of his virtual presence grew.

So sometime later, when a new Bishop was installed in Longford, I recognised him in media reports as Cahal Daly, the man I had not met in Belfast as a student. The historic bishopric included the townland of my paternal great-grandparents. My father inherited the old house and land there, and so my parents were regular visitors to the area. The local parish priest's housekeeper was a family connection, and a pattern of mutual visiting developed. Thus the stage was set for another near miss which happened when my parents reported one evening that they had visited the parish priest. Normally, the housekeeper allowed a bottle of Paddy or Power's whiskey to make an appearance, but on this occasion drink was off the agenda as the fledgling bishop was expected. The housekeeper felt that Bishop Daly might not approve. The prognosis proved correct and, to emphasize his position, the bishop even brought his own orange. Thereafter, I expected to encounter the bishop during one of many visits to my parents' retreat, but it never happened. And so, I continued to not meet Cahal Daly.

∞   ∞   ∞

Life rolled on and in 1982 the bishop was moved to Belfast. My next virtual encounter relates to this move, but I didn't become aware of it until ten more years had lapsed. It occurred when, with family members, we were reading through the papers of the recently deceased priest's housekeeper. We found the original of a speech, written in the housekeeper's unmistakable hand, to be given by the parish priest at a function to mark Cahal Daly's departure from Longford. By this time, he was Archbishop of Armagh, and a Cardinal. Again, I felt he had stolen a march on me.

Over the next decade, some curious force led me to muse, now and then, on whether he might have some awareness of me. Were we like 'ships that pass in the night'? The official meaning of the phrase refers to people who meet once briefly and pass by not to meet again. But I thought of it differently. It could mean ships that pass by without even being aware of each other. Or it could mean ships that pass, and one is aware of the encounter while the other isn't? Could he be aware of me, in an equally contrary way? Was I being stalked? Or was he avoiding me?

Again, life rolled on, the decade passed and then the answer came in a strange way. In 2004, the now retired cardinal published a book on environmental topics, *The Minding of Planet Earth*. It received good notices, and in many ways prefigured the concerns for the environment that are now part of common culture. While I didn't read the book, a friend sent me a copy of two pages from it that he felt I might find interesting. I was bowled over to see they contained reference to and quotations from an article I had published. So, there it was, after numerous false starts, I was as good as a virtual acquaintance of the late scholarly but remote cardinal.

∞   ∞   ∞

Being of a certain age and rather forgetful, I often use the strategy of hanging things not to be lost around my neck. I do this with keys but find an untrimmed length of rough twine does little for the dress sense and is unacceptable, even in academic circles. It is too close to the farmers of old, who not wishing to waste money on belt or braces, used a piece of rope to secure their trousers and avoid frightening the horses.

My adult children encouraged me to acquire a Fitbit. The model current at that time was a device about the size of a memory stick and was used to estimate the number of steps walked every day. This turned out to be a compelling motivator and I often go for a walk to make up the deficit, if the recommended target of 10,000 steps has not been reached.

The device is, like keys, prone to getting lost. So I acquired a nice trimmed black cord, attached the Fitbit to it, and wore it around my neck. Problem solved, or so it seemed for a few days at least. Shortly thereafter, I visited Worth Benedictine Abbey near London. The Abbot at the time, Christopher Jameson, made a practice of greeting each visitor on the way into the refectory for the evening meal. His eyes lit up when he spotted the Fitbit suspended around my neck, and immediately drew a parallel with his own pectoral Cross.

'Ah!' he said. 'Much better than a medal or a scapular! I see you are sporting a votive device to the font of all wisdom.' And I agreed.

Back home, a new problem appeared, as with a black cord and black Fitbit, it was easy to discard both into the laundry basket with a dark coloured shirt. The Fitbit didn't respond well to the washing machine. The solution was a bright gold coloured cord from Hickey's fabric and haberdashery shop in Dublin. It was almost luminous and hence never found its way into the laundry basket.

One fine September afternoon, I decided to walk a few circuits around the rose garden in St Anne's Park to add to the number of steps already achieved. The gardener was tending to the grass near the beginning of the walk, and we greeted each other. I walked at leisure, pausing to admire and smell the roses, many of which were still in bloom. Two elderly ladies engaged in animated conversation passed by, but once out of earshot they glanced back in my direction repeatedly. On completion of a circuit, the gardener waved and beckoned me to come over to where he was working. I approached aware that he was observing me a little too closely.

'Are you,' he asked tentatively, 'a bishop?' I was more than a little surprised.

'A bishop?' I responded. 'Absolutely not. Who gave you that idea?'

'You see the two women there,' he said, pointing at the two women ahead on the path. 'They think you are and stopped to ask me for your particulars.'

I was confused and couldn't fathom what might have led to such an enquiry. After all, in well over 70 years no one had accused me of holding episcopal rank before. Perhaps being a little on the well-nourished side might be responsible? After all, one seldom met a thin bishop – the adjective was reserved for forlorn-looking cardiologists and the otherwise anorexic. Shortly thereafter, a second sighting of the putative bishop occurred in a dimly lit restaurant. Diners a few tables away asked the waiter to enquire from our table who the bishop was and to wish him well. Again, I was mystified. Then it happened a third time, and on this occasion, I put two and two together and realised it must be the new bright gold cord and the Fitbit. In the distance they appeared like a gold chain and pectoral cross.

I reverted to the black cord and was more careful with the laundry. Accusations of being a bishop ceased and so did a clerical fascination. What a relief.

Chapter Three

Merriman, Merri-men, Merri-women: The Irish Summer School Experience

Useless to think you will pause
and capture it more thoroughly.

– Seamus Heaney, 'Postscript'

Decamping to one of the many beautiful locations on the west coast can, even in high summer, be risky weather-wise. But summer schools, with an abundance of activities including talks, walks, cultural events, music sessions, as well as hospitable pubs, restaurants, and cafés, ensure enjoyable days and nights. My most enduring experience of the genre is the Merriman, one of the first and among the best. Later, I was involved with the Robert Boyle Summer School, which had its moments although it is more science-focused. But my first exposure was in the 1980s at the Willie Clancy School in Milltown Malbay in West Clare. We had rented a large old house outside the village that was almost identical to the parish house in *Father Ted*. It had large rooms, small windows, thick walls and an incipient background of damp, characteristic of big old houses.

The Willie Clancy School starts on the first Saturday in July and lasts for a long week, extending over both weekends. The dress sense ranged from Irish Coastal Summer (including sandals with socks) to ageing hippy complete with pungent odour. I attended some of the numerous events, looked in at others and was unexpectedly drawn into a life-changing experience. Walking to the national school at ten in the morning to attend fiddle lessons was enjoyable. On entering, one encountered a wall of sound from instruments being tuned up, people playing while waiting for class, and individuals and teachers sharing tunes. This is pleasant in the memory, but it is unlikely to have been so at the time, particularly in the morning. About a hundred instruments were competing throughout the building, with ten to twenty in each room. The aspirant musicians were aged from seven to eighty, all sizes, shapes, nationalities and multiple genders, some of which had not yet reached public awareness. And for some attendees, it is not surprising the event came to be known as Willie Week.

The tutors were experienced traditional musicians giving generously of their time, and in some cases genius. Many were well known from radio and TV, as the music was enjoying a revival at the time. I first saw Martin Hayes there when he was a young man in his twenties, often accompanied by his father, the patriarch of the then almost fifty-year-old Tulla Céilí Band, which is still going strong. Martin went on to a stellar international career as a performer and innovator. The figures I now find most memorable are a few who played less than perfectly for the modern ear and include weather-beaten old men like John Kelly and Junior Creehan. Both were approaching the end of their days and were fiddle players with exceptional phrasing, rhythm and a great collection of tunes. Neither seemed concerned about concert pitch, something they had little need for during most of their lives. The uninitiated often only saw that they, and some pipers, played out of tune. But their music was special, and they were living archives of a great tradition. On the other hand, the elderly and gentle Micho Russel captivated with in-tune West Clare reels on the tin whistle.

By the morning tea break, people in every room were practicing tunes. Teachers and students spread out and found every available nook in the building. Favoured students were accompanied by tutors playing phrases from tunes on violins, concertinas, accordions, harps and flutes, creating a medley, or was it a cacophony? On entering the toilets, one morning, I was greeted by the sight of a student poised with violin in one cubicle, with the door propped open, and bravely attempting phrases from a difficult reel. His teacher paced the space out-side, offering advice and demonstration.

The music classes are a surreal and happy memory, but for me set dancing proved to be more enduring and life changing (Chapter Eleven). Here, it is sufficient to say that I had not pre-viously encountered the raw energy of full-on Clare set danc-ing until a memorable side event at the Willie Clancy School. Thereafter, from age about 40, I was captivated and acquired a new mission in life: to become a passable set dancer. In the language of the trade, a person with this level of proficiency is referred to as a tidy dancer. I achieved this accolade over a decade or so with the help of Mary Friel, Irene Martin, Eileen O'Doherty (and many others) at the Brooks Academy in Dub-lin, and the legendary Connie Ryan and his dancing/business partner, Betty McCoy, at various venues. The name Brooks Academy was a light-hearted reference to Christy Moore's rendering of the song 'Lanigan's Ball'. You could spend 'six months at Brooks Academy, learning the steps for Lanigan's Ball'.

∞   ∞   ∞

The Merriman Summer School was usually located in West Clare, about ten miles from Willie Clancy's home. An urban myth has it that the organisers of the first school (1967) wanted something to challenge the Yeats School in Sligo, which they felt was too academic and exclusive. While this may not be quite true, it captures something of the spirit that eventually came to animate the schools. They involved academics, but also enthusiastically welcomed journalists, writers, teachers and, most important, the plain people of Ireland, especially those from Clare. In other words, all of those interested in the world around them and the issues of the day.

The school was named after Brian Merriman, a late eighteenth century poet and mathematics teacher with origins in Clare. Unlike Yeats, he wrote only one poem that was cheeky or, in the vernacular, a dirty one. It is a romp from first to last, celebrating a mythic Rabelaisian eighteenth century Midnight Court convened by Aoibhall, the court's judge and monster fairy queen. She charges Irish men with failure to do their duty by the women of the country in a sense not spoken of in polite company. The court of women brings forward various characters including some miserable men and young women lamenting Ireland's falling population and the scarcity of partners able to deliver. The few available men wait until they are too old to satisfy young women. Among the proposals are that the big beefy priests throughout the country should marry regardless of anything coming from Rome. A bailiff summons various women to chastise Merriman himself and to show no mercy.

Over and above its literary worth, the poem is full of information about eighteenth century life, marriage, sex, population issues, birth outside marriage, clerical celibacy, women's rights, spells and cures. All of these were good topics for late night conversations that often continued into the morning – a hallmark of this school. Pre-famine sensibilities in Ireland seem greatly at variance with what emerged during the latter part of the nineteenth and much of the twentieth centuries. The poem was written and published in Irish. A few innocent opening verses were still on the Irish language curriculum when I was at school. But they gave little sense of the rollicking energy, rhythm and glee of the epic that followed. Many good translations are available including a partial one by Seamus Heaney. The two I like best are those by Frank O'Connor and Ciaran Carson. Carson's is more recent and is associated with the bicentenary of Merriman's death in 2005. It retains the original exuberance, wit and mixture of high rhetoric with rude colloquial. For most of the school's life Frank O'Connor's was the most accessible. Extracts follow, first from O'Connor's:

> *Has the Catholic Church a glimmer of sense*
> *That the priests won't marry like anyone else?*
> *Is it any wonder the way I am,*
> *Out of my mind for the want of a man,*
> *When there's men by the score with looks and leisure,*
> *Walking the roads and scorning pleasure?*
> *The full of a fair of primest beef,*
> *Warranted to afford relief,*
> *Cherry-red cheeks and bull-like voices,*
> *And bellies dripping with fat in slices,*
> *Backs erect and heavy hind quarters,*

Hot-blooded men, the best of partners,
Freshness and charm, youth and good looks
And nothing to ease their mind but books!
The best fed men that travel the country,
Beef and mutton, game and poultry,
Whiskey and wine forever in stock,
Sides of bacon, beds of flock.
Mostly they're hardy under the hood,
And we know like ourselves that they're flesh and blood;
I wouldn't ask much of the old campaigners,
The good-for-nothings and born complainers,
But petticoat-tossers aloof and idle
And fillies gone wild for bit and bridle!

To top this off he comforts us with the thought that the Church may well be considering lifting the ban on clerical celibacy, and this at the end of the eighteenth century. The few who are still interested wait in vain. This is from Carson's translation:

A rumour I heard, that I put to one side,
For the gab of old women I cannot abide;
It's button your lip, keep your eye on the ball,
And whatever you say, say nothing at all!
But beware of the wiles of the powers that be,
For the word is the clergy will marry, you'll see!
And committees in Rome will approve a decree,
Which the Pope will endorse with the seal of the See;
That given the desperate state of the nation,
Priests should combine against depopulation –
Big fellows, with plenty of kick,
Who'll do as you please, and you'll each have your pick.

Those involved with the school from the early days included a remarkable cross section of Irish life, like David Greene (Professor of Irish at Trinity College Dublin); Donal Foley (*The Irish Times*); Seán J. White (public servant, writer, academic, broadcaster); Con Howard of the Department of Foreign Affairs; and Liam Ó Dochartaigh (University of Limerick). Ciarán Mac Mathúna, Sean Mac Réamoinn, Diarmuid Breathnach and Bob Collins (all RTÉ) were also involved. Maeve Binchy, Nuala O'Faolain, Mary Kenny, Marian Finucane and Nell McCafferty were among the supporters of the feminist movement that were to be found there every year. And there were of course many others, including the set dancing team and musicians.

The school was conducted in a holiday atmosphere which allowed the exceptional and inspired to happen. For example, a well-known journalist and writer, responding from the floor to a speaker, declared she didn't have the language to explain whatever was involved. But, she continued, she would sing part of a song that would make the point. And she did – to an awesome stillness – as it was something that could have gone very wrong. And it did make everything plain in a way speech could never have achieved.

The inspiring academic programme on each year's theme was embedded in an infrastructure that reflected this priority and carried over from year to year. It included classes, workshops, and an exhausting and often liquid-fuelled social programme. Set dancing started in the 1980s and was under the direction of dance master Connie Ryan and Betty McCoy. After Connie's death, Johnny Morrissey filled his shoes literally and figuratively. And all of this was rounded off by something special, a poetry reading on the final morning (of which more below). The activities started about 9.30 am and did not finish until the small hours of the following morning. The formal elements were garnished with music, dancing, song and recitations, most of which were provided by the participants. Late-night song and conversation could last until dawn. On the way to breakfast, it was not uncommon to meet stragglers from last night's fun. This magic web was the product of a committed group of organisers. It seemed the month of August drew it from them as a natural part of summer's decline.

Formal lecture slots at the school were normally 45 minutes or so and the discussion afterwards often went on for an hour. However, the lectures were not the normal PowerPoint framed academic talk. For most of its half century PowerPoint and slides were frowned on. The lecture was the person, their thoughts, insights and charisma; hiding behind slides was discouraged. For many, this was a terrifying challenge. An invitation to give a Merriman lecture was an honour but was also a way of destroying a summer. Likewise, an invitation to direct the school signalled recognition, but it was also a challenge, and a way of destroying a whole year.

I directed two schools, and while chuffed to be invited I experienced the intimidating weight of expectation. In the dark winter prior to announcing the programme, there were times when I almost despaired of getting the right mixture of speakers, each with some exceptional expertise and able to deliver a memorable and inspiring lecture without slides or other AV crutches. Even when a coterie of performers with these qualities had been assembled, it had to survive the scrutiny of the inevitable committees – not always easy to secure. But in Merriman, they were open, up to a point, and persuadable, also up to a point. I was often surprised at how supportive of innovation Ciarán Mac Mathúna was. He could seem to be asleep at the table and would then interject quietly and firmly in favour of whatever was being debated. And that was the end of the matter. But there were boundaries. For example, inviting Roddy Doyle to speak was rejected because one Dublin academic did not regard his work as literature and could not live with the prospect. Though this view was not shared by others in the committee, we did not go ahead with the proposal.

Organising any event like this involves dealing with the great and the good and mistakes are inevitable. I recall capturing, just in time, an email to the newly appointed Archbishop of Dublin, Diarmuid Martin, in which the primitive spell checker replaced *Dear Diarmuid* with *Dear Dairymaid*. Perhaps potentially more embarrassing was an email from a speaker with a draft manuscript of his talk. He wished to check if it would work at the school. I was in my office in St James's Hospital with half an hour to spare before a meeting in the medical school. So I printed the talk without looking through it, scribbled my name on the first page and went to a coffee shop upstairs in the entrance lobby that offered an uninterrupted reading opportunity.

The manuscript dealt with previously unpublished letters from Joyce to his wife Nora, which had just become available. They were essentially private communications and had long passages of the most explicit, graphic, and scatological descriptions of sexual fantasies that separated lovers might dream up, including some that were new to me. Joyce scholars were avidly interested in every detail, but would it work at the school? It might be okay in the cold, clinical atmosphere of an academic conference, but could be embarrassing for participants at Merriman, who shared a different relaxed form of intimacy.

The available half hour was up and so gathering up my papers, I moved on to the medical school meeting. Sometime into the meeting, it gradually dawned on me that the Joyce manuscript was missing. I checked several times and yes, it was missing. Where could it be? My name was scribbled on top, and the author had not included his name. Was it left on the table in the café? Or dropped while walking? Panic! Anyone finding it and glancing through could conclude I was the author of this powerful fantasy. What to do? I quickly excused myself and raced back to the café. And what a relief: it was still sitting undisturbed on the table which had not yet been cleared. Eventually, a version of the paper was given and later published, moderated a little so as not to make everybody too uncomfortable, but not enough to lose its impact. A few were inevitably uncomfortable and let it be known. There was more than the usual amount of chat about it afterwards.

Academic strife and near misses aside, the product was generally a week with an excellent programme embedded in broader discussion of the weather, poetry, music, as well as the conviviality, singing and set dancing in the local pubs that made the school what it was.

While directing a school could steal a year, it had its luminous moments and two are related here. The first, in 2001, was on the apparently impenetrable topic of the school, 'Research and Discovery: Of Knowledge and the People' (the first part was wonderfully translated to Irish as: *Slí an Eolais*). Many regulars were concerned that the title might put people off. But equally, others felt it would work, partly because the notion of the knowledge economy was in the air and Ireland's high participation rate in third level education had come of age.

After much discussion we secured the participation of poet/philosopher/mystic and former priest John O'Donoghue. As the school progressed, so did my concern for his session on the Thursday afternoon. His title, 'The Epistemology of the Imagination', was not likely to be a crowd puller. Even more worrying was the weather which had settled into a pattern of beautiful late summer days, brilliant blue skies and high temperatures. The sea and the local beaches at Spanish Point, Lahinch and Fanore beckoned. For those not so inclined, the risk of drought mandated prophylactic afternoon visits to one or more of the area's welcoming pubs. I thought, right up to the time of the lecture, that John's audience might only be a few committee members. But I need not have worried. The sun still shone brilliantly, but against all the odds several hundred people flowed in.

The crowd was silenced by John's mellifluous, deep, sonorous Clare voice; his lecture was a symphony of ideas, one of the exceptional talks of the schools of that period. Later we congratulated ourselves on forfeiting the weather and celebrated our good fortune. A participant gave me a CD of the event, and twenty years on it retains its appeal, especially as John has died since.

∞   ∞   ∞

A second memorable occasion involved Professor Patrick Crotty, a notable contributor and facilitator at the year 2000 school. He made the forgivable error of trying to participate in too much, and as the week progressed appeared a little strained, but was still able to cope. Toward the end of the week, I had a short slot before the evening lecture to promote the following year's school and sat waiting for him to give me the floor.

That year, I was accompanied by some family and a group of friends from Trinity and St James's Hospital. The latter included three thirty-something women from medical physics and Professor Michael Walsh, a distinguished cardiologist, who has since passed. The ladies knew how to make an entrance, partied at any hour, and the previous evening had joined in all the activities of the school including an elaborate dinner, the evening lecture and discussion that went on until 10.30 pm. After that they continued to Club Merriman at which there was set dancing, music and song until 1.00 am. Finally, they adjourned to a *lock-in* pub session for more song and discussion on the troubled subjects of the day and the meaning of life. Professor Crotty had accompanied the ladies and Professor Walsh on this marathon, but I wisely departed at 1.00 am when the dancing finished. On the following evening, when he came to introduce my small promotion, he was ashen. As he went to the podium the ladies, looking spectacular, made an entrance and caught his eye. He paused, consulted his notes, sighed and wistfully announced:

'This year's school is moving to its conclusion – we have only a day left. Can I survive? First, this evening, Jim Malone will give you a preview of next year's school. He is, as many of you know, from TCD and St James's Hospital. But you may not know that he is accompanied by the *marauding band of female physicists* that have just joined us. They live in the fast lane. Not only do they dance till 1.00 am, but afterwards they adjourn to Lynch's lounge, where the difference between night and day is not taken seriously.'

'And, as we can see, they emerge fragrant for this evening's new challenge,' he continued, pointing at the ladies, with Professor Walsh bringing up the rear. 'How do they do this?' I ask myself. Well, about 3.00 am this morning, I discovered their secret. You see, the gentleman of mature years accompanying them is their travelling cardiologist, whose constant attention keeps them going. That's how they do it!' And that was more memorable than anything I said about the next school – or anything mentioned by the speaker that followed.

∞ ∞ ∞

My memories of arriving at a Merriman consistently have an almost surreal quality, in which the weather is good, and the welcome is special. Here is the rosy picture I allow myself to indulge: it is a warm, late August evening, freshened by a light breeze. Lisdoonvarna, known for matchmaking, is hosting the event. My maternal grandfather, a farmer, regularly visited it in the early part of the twentieth century in search of diversion once the harvest was over. I park at the end of the town; it would be competitive at the venue and would disrupt the benign mood fostered by the weather and the occasion. The steep incline to the valley is welcoming, with old friends negotiating the steps, some now with walking sticks. The evening sun sparkles on the windows of the Pumphouse and the event building – three sides of glass – a large jewel embedded in the centre of a lush valley. The low point is about the size of a football pitch, half stolen by the centre and a lawn. The other half – wooded with mature trees and shrubs in their prime, uncharacteristic of West Clare – offers a secret oasis with heady evening scents and shelter from Atlantic storms.

People are gathering and greeting each other while strolling toward the centre, its open reception area of scrubbed pine and glass is welcoming. A few old friends and acquaintances are relaxing on seats on the lawn and inside at the coffee bar. Two are studiously examining the progress of the stream from the small decorative humpback bridge. I drift toward the coffee bar, where honest, slightly inefficient hospitality always takes a little longer than it should, acquire a cup of tea and move toward the function room. Una Quinn, Merriman's secretary, is energetically welcoming and delaying all at the rickety improvised registration desk with a Mother's Union cash box. But what a welcome. She could make the devil himself and all his fallen angels feel at home in the company of saints.

Inside, the centre is a dramatic rectangular space, with an elevated stage and inclined ceiling. One side, almost completely glass, opens onto the mature trees and shrubs that the sun will charm with changing hues as the evening advances and the light begins to fail. I place my tea and book on a chair near the window as a place holder. The other side of the room faces on to the open expanse of lawn, a small stream and the buzz of people gathering to hear something special.

There is a scent of flowers from arrangements strategically placed near the stage. It is accompanied by an undertone of wax polish disguising a hint of damp and locker room from the energetic midday set dance workshop. The fine wooden floor had enjoyed a rare exposure to the dancing feet it was made for. Now it is hidden by over 350 chairs put out and arranged in neat rows. Incisive TV commentator and academic, the late Brian Farrell, always observed that 'the best test of a dedicated committee member is one 'who's willing to put out the chairs' – 'like someone you can rely on to close the gate on a field of cattle.' How true! The reverie is interrupted as people began to drift to their seats, many recognisable figures, in search of something beyond being busy and successful. I drift to my seat again, anticipating being enveloped in the mood of what is to pass on the stage while outside, the sun will sink gradually until the trees become ghosts of themselves.

It's a full house with people standing around the edge – the great, the good and the citizens of West Clare. Many are catching up from last year – news, romances, break-ups, births, deaths and so on. And people who are known for something special or memorable interventions. Like Mattie the Post from East Galway who would decisively undermine even a hint of self-importance in a speaker that misjudges this odd occasion as one for academic point scoring. Some well-known political journalists take places in the front row. Other media people, prominent figures from the diplomatic circuit and mandarins from the department of Foreign Affairs and Taoiseach's Department join the crowd, filter in and try to go unnoticed. Obviously, something important is expected, and I am blissfully unaware of it. The speaker is Edna O'Brien, the novelist.

Edna is ceremoniously escorted to the stage by the chairman for the evening. She looks tall, in a formal dark dress, appears nervous, willowy, fragile and younger than her years. A hush runs through the room, and the speaker is formally introduced. The year is 1994, four years before the Good Friday Agreement and scarcely a month before the broadcasting ban was lifted on Sinn Féin, still the great untouchables. Edna speaks intensely, with a studied breathlessness, and with characteristic deliberation, about her 1994 novel, *House of Splendid Isolation*. It explores the Troubles, putting together an IRA man on the run and the elderly woman in whose home he takes refuge. The presentation is compelling, if on the wrong side of the strained political correctness of the time. I settle into this, forgetting the diplomatic invasion witnessed earlier. She diverts to talk about a favourable profile of Gerry

Adams that she has just published in *The New Yorker*, and a palpable shiver runs through the room. Clearly the heavy hitters are preparing to respond. The talk lasts less than an hour, and following nervous applause the chair invites questions and comments. A slight, fragile, fey Edna O'Brien waits for the response from a room colonised by heavyweight commentators and diplomats.

And then it happens! A debate in which the great and the good, politicians, diplomats, journalists, in effect the establishment heavies – many are big beefy men – attack a slight, dignified, vulnerable-looking woman for publishing what they refused to publish and for writing what they were afraid to write. What a debate, and what an occasion to have witnessed. And the slight, dignified, vulnerable-looking woman not only holds her ground, but clearly wins the day as she did over thirty years earlier, when the establishment exiled her and banned her first three novels, now almost universally celebrated.

It is surprising that an event such as Merriman escaped being written about in fiction, especially as it was patronised by so many writers, journalists and broadcasters. It was reported in detail in the broadsheets and on the radio from the 1980s for about a quarter of a century. But I have been able to find only three literary works that make more than a passing reference to it. *Irish Times* columnist Nuala O'Faolain's hugely successful and heart-breaking memoir *Are You Somebody?* featured it. Maeve Binchy wrote a hilarious short story about it and there is reference to it in a novel by broadcaster and anchor of the morning news programme on RTÉ 1, David Hanley. Perhaps the others treasured it in their private thoughts and felt it would go on for ever.

The last Summer School, the 49th, commemorated the centenary of the 1916 rising, and ended almost half a century of an outstanding reflective institution. For those involved, it had been an occasion of learning, reflection, mischief, craic, the companionship of kindred spirits and of course laughter in abundance. They spread their wings each day, if only to swim from one of the beaches, explore and wander a little in the Burren or relax in one (or more) of the many fine pubs in the area. It had the quality of an unorthodox retreat from the preoccupations of daily life, was often transformative and a wellspring for personal development. It gave us the opportunity to 'Walk on air, against our better judgment,' to misquote Seamus Heaney's line and epitaph. Its demise was a big loss, and even though its dying was protracted, many hoped against hope for its survival. Unsurprisingly, it took some time before those involved were ready and able to celebrate its demise, as well as its wonderful successes.

Eventually, in November 2019, Aideen Friel and Treasa Mac Mánais organised a dinner at the Arts Club in Dublin, scene of many AGMs, at which it was possible to enjoy reminiscing and celebrate the wonderful thing we had shared. The occasion was a one for hilarious recollections, many of which are unrepeatable, and not a few about those who are no longer with us. Perhaps just one (or two) tales here! From its early days, Con Howard was an exceptional presence at the school. He had been a senior figure in the Department of Foreign Affairs and an endless source of inspiration and ideas. Not given to systematic management he could, tornado-like, unwittingly leave a trail of chaos and collateral damage. When he died and the occasion came to pause to honour his memory, it was solemnly (and appropriately) proposed that, perhaps, one minute's silence was not quite right. Two minutes of pande-monium would be much more appropriate! How true.

There was something Rabelaisian about him. I recall a morning when on the way to breakfast in the hotel, Con erupted from his room. He was still in last night's outfit, jacket askew, straining shirt buttons unsuccessfully trying to contain his considerable bulk. And the shirt itself flapping in the flatulent wind in a manner that Boris Johnson could only aspire to. When we reached the breakfast room, he nodded with an air of urgent desperation and a readiness to flirt with anyone showing signs of a pulse. He had spotted the three young women from St James's Hospital sitting chatting ani-matedly in the morning sunshine at a distant table near the window. He confided to me, 'I need a woman!' and eyeing the three continued, 'what do you think?' I nodded in apprehen-sion, but need not have worried as he was quickly distracted by the breakfast buffet.

∞   ∞   ∞

Even though Merriman emerged from a single poem, the school had a special place for poetry. On the final Saturday morning at about 11.00 am the survivors of the week and of Friday night's deliberations gathered, usually in a large func-tion room of a local hotel. The atmosphere was hushed with a feeling of expectation shared by the gathered poets, poetry aficionados, and many who prior to their Merriman connec-tion had little interest in poetry. This ninety-minute event became the jewel in the crown of the school; nothing before it and nothing after compared, other than goodbyes and look-ing forward to the next year: *go mbeirimíd beo ar an am seo arís*. It had a unique structure; most of the readings were by two presenters rather than the original authors or poets. For decades, Sean Mac Réamoinn, a father figure of thoughtful radio programmes, presided. He had a deep, resonant voice and the intellectual and emotional intelligence to carry off such an occasion. And despite decades of experience he was nervous, like a bag of cats for days before the event. Later the baton passed to others including Doireann Ní Bhriain and Eoghan Ó hAnluain. The script for these occasions was prepared throughout the year by Diarmuid Breathnach and Mary Murphy, formerly of the library in RTÉ. They sensitively and expertly excavated wonderful material that connected the theme of the year's school, its speakers and the participants. It became an enchanted coda to the week.

The school formed special relationships with many poets and a regular, well-attended event in later years was a Cúirt an Mheán Lea (a mid-day visit) when a poet was invited to read their work every day, for about an hour before lunchtime and the set dancing workshop. This was extremely popular and added to the list of the many distinguished poets who had contributed to the school over its half century.

The school had a special place for Seamus Heaney, who reciprocated by becoming its Patron. He was a regular contributor, and always drew a large crowd. Possibly surprisingly for one so experienced on the world stage, he was often extremely nervous. The final time we saw him was in a shed in a small business park in Lisdoonvarna in what became a magical evening. He had agreed to read at an event to end the 2013 school on Friday, August 16. He was accompanied by his friend, the poet Michael Longley. They often read together at functions across the world and were at ease with each other. Both were in their seventies, at the top of their game, and on this occasion Heaney was relaxed with little trace of the nervousness that often accompanied his performances. There was a stillness, a silence, a rapt attention in the room. The alternation of voices from one poem to the next gave just enough variety, and after about an hour or so, the performance moved gently to what we presumed was the end, although we wished it could last forever.

And then without warning the room erupted as a group of elaborately masked and costumed traditional musicians and singers emerged from every corner in a what would now be called a pop-up event. They transformed the reflective mood into one of an almost pagan celebration of the human spirit. The Armagh Rhymers (akin to Mummers and Wren boys) enthralled with their quasi-ritual performance. Their traditional masks, costumes, drama, song and music brought a special evening to a natural close and removed from the poets the strain of ending something unfinishable. Just two weeks later, on August 30, Seamus Heaney died at Blackrock Clinic, after falling while leaving a restaurant the evening before. We were, on that evening in Lisdoonvarna, to repeat his own words, 'walking on air, against our better judgment'. But we were the better for it. And, for me, the Merriman School also died on that luminous evening.

Chapter Four

When Things Go Wrong:
A Hot Dentist, a Cool Student,
and a Troubled Hospital

A little learning is a dangerous thing.
– Alexander Pope

Fools rush in where angels fear to tread.
– Alexander Pope

Professors and academics are often asked to help sort things out when they go astray. The covid pandemic provides an example of this on a grand scale. Professors are the lifeblood of universities, and the universities are the carriers of a deep and broad knowledge of many if not most areas of life. They should also be, at least in theory, detached from the cauldron of vested interests that are part and parcel of daily life. In this chapter we look at examples of situations where somethings were frankly wrong and how a professor became involved in their resolution. In Chapter Ten we look at a different type of situation where professors can also find themselves involved.

Initial inklings of the first case started with a phone call from a general practitioner in Galway. We will refer to him as 'Dr Amber'. He was upset and gave the impression that he was having difficulty finding somebody to lend him an ear. One of his patients, a dentist in his thirties, had persistent signs of illness that weren't clearing up. He felt the explanation could be that he (the dentist) was accidentally radiated. I heard him out and, once he had settled down, he came across as a reasonable person with an unsolved problem that was worrying him. Even if he was overreacting, he needed help and I decided to investigate more fully.

I arranged to see Dr Amber some time later in his surgery. He was slim, of medium height and about my own age (approximately 40 at the time). He was wearing a well-cut suit and I seem to remember a waistcoat. His surgery occupied a fine old house in The Crescent, a good suburb of Galway city. His manner was that of an earnest, socially concerned and successful practitioner. His core message was that the dentist had consulted him about a variety of symptoms including abdominal pains, nausea and vomiting. Initially, these were attributed to modest indulgence in Guinness and oysters, which were plentiful at the time. However, the symptoms didn't clear up as one would have expected. The dentist mentioned that they might be due to an accident that could have involved radiation that occurred some weeks earlier. Dr Amber was anxious that the situation be investigated. With hindsight, Dr Amber's initiative not only addressed the dentist's problem: it also had a significant, unacknowledged impact on improving dental practice throughout the country.

Shortly thereafter, I visited the dentist and his assistant at their public surgery which was owned by the Western Health Board. It was attractive, newly equipped and in a well furbished building. Both the dentist and his assistant were pleasant and helpful. They were informally dressed, relaxed and anxious to get to the bottom of the problem. Both were concerned about their own health and that of their families as some of the symptoms had not yet cleared up. It took quite a while to assemble a clear account of the incident. Here is a summary of what happened, which was subsequently published in *The Irish Times* during legal proceedings:

> *The incident involved a brand-new dental X-ray set which had been installed in a newly equipped and commissioned dental surgery. The suppliers, a well-known company in the dental market, installed the machine on the instructions of the Western Health Board. X-ray machines were a normal part of dental practice at the time. Toward the end of the week prior to the opening of the new facility, the dentist and his assistant visited the surgery to ensure everything, including the equipment, would be ready for patients on the following Monday. As part of this exercise, all the new equipment was plugged in including the X-ray set. Normally the latter will only emit X-rays when a hand switch is depressed and, even then, only momentarily.*
>
> *The dentist and the assistant checked that everything expected had been delivered and was in working order. The dentist elevated the patient chair and was using it as a worktop on which he spread out manuals, instructions and small pieces of equipment. The head of the X-ray unit was above and behind him directed down toward the table. After about 90 minutes the dentist became aware of a humming sound that he had assumed was coming from a light fitting somewhere in the room. At about the same time he noticed the head of the X-ray unit was hot. In retrospect it seems that it had been continually producing X-rays since it was plugged in. He had been quite close to it for the entire period and the assistant though also present in the room was some distance away. He confirmed it had been emitting X-rays, by momentarily exposing an X-ray*

Making a long forgotten point

Lesley Malone, circa 1980s

Preparing for a session at Merriman, early 2000s

Clockwise from front left, my mother Nancy, a friend, the author
and (daughter) Fran, lunch during Willie Clancy week, 1994

Mickey Kelly (Dancer Master), Una Quinn (Merriman secretary),
Diarmuid Breathnach (RTÉ and former Merriman Chairman),
Eoin O'hAnluian (UCD) at Merriman, 1993

Louis O'Rourke (Bray Set Dancers) and Maeve Binchy at Merriman, 1996

Preparing radioactive injections, Meath Hospital, 1980s
– not quite as it is done today

JJ and Nancy, happy in the breakfrast room

Dad (JJ) with grandsons Conor and John F. near Ireland's Eye, 1987

(Son) Professor David Malone appears in Maynooth campus poster, 2019

Portrait by Des Hickey in TCD Medical School, circa 2004

Kieran Taaffe and Brid Anne Ryan on each side of portrait.
Artist Scientists Des Hickey and Tommy Scott on the right, circa 2004

Easter Lunch with family and visitors at Berry Lodge in West Clare 1996
From left: (son) David, friend, (friend of Fran) Doaky, (mother) Nancy,
(wife of Frank) Bernie Malone, the author, Lesley Malone, (brother)
Frank Malone RIP, Aran Quigley, and (daughter) Fran Malone.

Letting go with dancing partner at retirement party, Gerry Ryan in background

film to the beam. He unplugged the machine, the buzzing stopped, and it cooled down. The supplier was contacted and asked to correct the fault before the following Monday so that the clinic could open as planned.

On Monday, the dentist came to the surgery and assumed the machine had been fixed. He confirmed this to his own satisfaction. The first patient to be X-rayed was a child. He positioned the X-Ray machine above the child, and instead of using the exposure hand switch, he decided to switch the machine on and off quickly using the switch on the wall socket at which it was plugged in. As he did so, the machine exploded. The head disintegrated and the room was sprayed with cooling oil. The child sat up and the head came down hitting the chair where the patient had been.

Following the incident, no formal reports were made to the Health Board or the radiation licencing authority. However, over the next three to five weeks both the dentist and the assistant experienced a variety of symptoms including severe abdominal pain, nausea and vomiting. He also, then and/or later, experienced more localised symptoms in the shoulder, hands, mouth and eyes. These led to the consultation with Dr Amber who initiated the investigations of the equipment and the circumstances.

The equipment investigation revealed a simple defect that had caused the accident. The hand-switch controlling exposures was bypassed. As a result, the mains supply was directly connected to the X-ray generating system once the device was plugged in to a live socket. This was only possible because of a serious design flaw, which was later reported to the standards organisation for all electrical/medical equipment. The fact that the Health Board allowed such dangerous equipment to be installed and used without being verified to be safe by somebody independent of the supplier was also regarded as a serious problem. The Radiological Protection Institute of Ireland (RPII) became involved and undertook its own investigation as did the Chief Dental Officer of the Department of Health. The net result was that new guidelines were developed for the use of radiation equipment in dentistry. This, with the co-operation of dentists throughout the country, greatly improved safety in the area, and is a good example of how one event, well followed up and analysed, can have a significant impact on many lives.

The dentist had received significant exposures. The largest dose was to his right shoulder, but there were also signs of significant exposures to his upper right arm, posterior head and neck, lungs, trunk, right hand and right thigh. The consequences included temporary opacity in the right eye, the gastrointestinal symptoms referred to above, lesions in the mouth and several skin lesions. In addition, there was an estimated 1 per cent risk of a serious cancer. The assistant received much less exposure, but developed thyroid problems, which may or may not have been connected. Both suffered persistent anxiety that was not alleviated by their professional knowledge and training. They had to suffer a long period of intrusive and invasive medical follow up which, while helpful, carries its own inconvenience and discomfort. The dentist acquired a lasting phobia to radiography which intruded on his subsequent professional life.

The incident became the subject of legal proceedings in the High Court in Dublin. The case went to trial but was stopped on the second day, as it was clear which way it was going. The settlement with the dentist and his assistant was not revealed but was known to be substantial. The suppliers took the hit and the Health Board escaped liability. In my opinion that was an unfair distribution of blame and several other incidents later came to light that confirmed this. But that is the way the pieces fell on the day. Fair or otherwise, the incident had an exceptional impact during the following decade on the practice of dentistry with respect to radiation. Parallel with this, there were moves to greatly improve infection control in dentistry and the improvements in both reinforced each other significantly.

With hindsight the improvements can be traced back to a small number of situations involving individuals who decided to do the troublesome *right thing* on occasions when it might have been easier not to do so. In this case, the credit goes to the diligence of Dr Amber, the medical physics follow up, and the diligence of the Chief Dental Officer in the Department of Health. All three, in a quiet way, significantly improved dentistry. The real cost of the improvement is not the additional spending involved in doing things properly, but in the damage to the life and careers of those unnecessarily exposed to radiation, particularly the dentist, and the many patients who had unwittingly paid the silent cost of less than satisfactory treatment.

On a different note, international students, for example from the Middle and Far East, often come to Ireland. Occasionally they can experience problems, some almost intractable, due to a lack of connectedness to local networks or lack of knowledge of how things work in their new environment. On the other hand, the problem may be related to where they have come from. For example, around the turn of the new century, we had many requests for admission from Iraqi refugees who had already completed several years in medical schools at home. But having escaped the troubled situation at home, they often found themselves without documentation, with no proof of results, and no hope of getting it in the foreseeable future. Many felt that the only response, in the circumstances, was to turn them away. But, in Trinity, on this occasion, we devised a process that, with assessment and interviews, allowed us to respond with humanity and confidence to such requests.

That is not to say that requests from students from less developed parts of the world are always worthy ones, as the following case illustrates. One Asian medical student, whom we will refer to as 'Madan Patel', was intelligent and charming, but he failed his exams every summer, and failed again at repeats later in the year. Each year, this should have been the end of the story – but he was well schooled in college regulations, entered a formal appeal every year and succeeded in winning. I encountered him after his failure in the repeat exams in the pre-final year. Again, this should have been the end of the road. However, he again appealed and requested that he be allowed to repeat again. A Faculty Appeal Board was assembled to deal with this and other difficult cases. It consisted of five or six experienced academics, supported by the Faculty Registrar. The student attended to make his case and was supported by his tutor, whose role was to act as an advocate on his behalf.

Madan and his advocate proceeded to give an account of the reasons for the current year's failures. It appears that he had been living in a noisy apartment and study had been difficult if not impossible. He had also been disorganised and less than diligent in his approach to work up to the summer. However, over the summer he had visited India and encountered a wise guru who introduced him to a well-ordered way of life. He was working well coming up to the autumn exams. And then came the *coup de grâce* to the unsympathetic board:

his dog died. He was so distraught that he couldn't do justice to the exams and requested an opportunity to repeat again. And all this was presented with solemn sincerity that gave no hint of the underlying dissimulation.

We recognised that people do experience grief at the loss of a pet, but Mr Patel's case was unconvincing. By his own account he had spent a fulfilling summer far from Dublin and the dog. The board unanimously rejected his appeal, only to have it accepted at a higher level in the college. So, he was back in business, with the opportunity to idle away another year or two. This example, and the Iraqi problem mentioned above, illustrate that there is a human side to how people are dealt with in what may appear to be the relatively detached and eccentric world of the Ivory Tower. Responding to such problems is part of the job, part of every day and, while it goes unsung, it consumes a lot of the time of many good academics. But it also makes it difficult to dispose of the occasional bad egg.

∞   ∞   ∞

The final incident in this chapter comes to mind when I think of an early autumn afternoon in West Clare, far from the stresses of Dublin. I was reading after lunch and settled comfortably on a recliner on a sun-trapping patio protected from the prevailing wind. Putting my novel down, I looked out to the ocean, and sipping a drink thought: It's Monday and by now they'll be going wild in the Department of Health and at the hospital (which will remain nameless) and I'm relaxed, uncontactable and away from it all.

It was mid-1990s and two weeks earlier problems at the hospital had reached a critical stage that could not be sidelined anymore. Several staff had departed, some voluntarily and others were pushed. The competence and safety of the cancer treatments delivered there were being called into question. The hospital claimed that all was well, but trust in such assurances was low. A senior civil servant from the Department of Health, whom we will refer to as 'Michael Dimond', phoned canvassing opinion on the situation. He was sceptical, perhaps bruised by scandals that were in the news at the time, particularly those involving blood products. I confirmed that it would be difficult to stand over the situation at the hospital in public. A few days later, he phoned again:

'Hello Professor Malone. Michael Dimond here. We considered the situation after the discussion the other day and it is being reviewed at the highest level. Would you be willing to take a look at the hospital and make recommendations on how things might be improved?'

'Have you spoken with the hospital about this?'

'Yes,' he replied. 'The board and the CEO would welcome your involvement.'

This was likely to be a poisoned chalice. Even with board approval, it was unlikely that the medical and professional staffs would give a wholehearted welcome to the level of external scrutiny involved. I played for time but didn't see a way of saying no; this was needed and long overdue.

'Michael, you've obviously been busy getting the ducks in a row. How about the medical and other professional staff?'

'They are a concern,' he replied. 'But the CEO and chairman feel they will be okay.'

'Can you check that the management will be able to deliver on this? If they can, I will do it, but if they can't or won't, it's very risky and may not work.'

And so I quickly found myself, against my better judgement, embroiled in a situation that proved to be more difficult, dangerous and unpleasant with each passing day. By the end of two weeks, it was clear that my initial reservations were well founded, and that the CEO and hospital board could not deliver the co-operation of the medical and professional staff. In addition, the Department of Health were less than energetic in underwriting their commitment. The situation was running aground, and two weeks later I left the hospital on a Friday after lunch looking for thinking space, retreated to Bewley's, and ruminated on what to do.

By 4.00 pm I had decided to withdraw with immediate effect. Walking across O'Connell Bridge to rescue my car I was looking for a working telephone box (this was prior to everyone having a mobile phone) and found one on Eden Quay.

'Can you put me on to Michael Dimond please?' I asked on getting through to the Department of Health.

'Sorry, he is not available just now,' the receptionist responded.

'Can you take a message for him?'

'Yes.'

'Tell him that Jim Malone called and sees no prospect of being able to deliver what the Minister needs. The professional and medical staff are not co-operating, and both the board and CEO have little influence on them. Regrettably, therefore, I am handing the task entrusted to me back incomplete. It needs a more robust intervention...'

Now, I thought, where to go to that isn't contactable for a while?

I headed for Clare, to an elevated west coast location above the ocean, a haven, a bolthole. The weekend was wonderful, good weather, lots of music and dancing in Vaughan's Barn in

Kilfenora, and by Sunday evening all thought of the Department of Health and the hospital had been erased. Given the good weather, taking Monday off provided the rest needed after the weekend's exertion, and sitting out on the recliner alternately reading and dozing was perfect therapy.

Glancing sideways toward the quiet, traffic-free back road to Spanish Point, a cyclist was progressing from the village. Where was she going as she edged along slowly? She was like the cursor on a sat nav; but there was not much for her to visit up here. She drew near and paused to consider the few houses that occupied the landscape. She resumed, progressed along the road, and turned into the pathway leading to my house. Must be looking for directions, I mused, and shortly thereafter heard the knock on the door. On opening it, a girl in her teens blurted:

'Are you the professor from Dublin?'

'I could be. Can I help?'

'I'm from down by the post office below,' she said. 'There's someone looking for ya on the public phone there, and they want to talk to a professor from Dublin who stays around here. Is it you, do ya think?'

So much for not being able to be contacted in the pre-mobile phone era. What to do? I was rumbled, and the healing solitude of the day quickly dispersed.

'It could be!'

'Will ya come down to the post office then?' she asked.

'I'll come when I'm not busy,' was the grumpy reply to the unfortunate girl, and she departed, making her way slowly back to the post office.

Later, after making peace with the intrusion, I went to the village, responded to the call and, predictably, was soon on the way back to the city and the problems and unpleasantness of the previous weeks.

Back in Dublin, the fray beckoned and by the following weekend it had ripened and become totally absorbing again. A sense of duty, given the right circumstances, can destroy peace of mind, undermine happiness, and disturb the composure of even the calmest temperaments. In this case the collateral damage extended from late summer until after Christmas. There were highs and lows and periods of intense engagement – not only with the management but also, now, with its more cooperative professionals. In addition, a host of other interests began to feature, including regulators, professional bodies, staff trade unions, civil servants, and finally inspectors from outside the country appointed by the local regulators. All with a view to getting the show safely back on the road and ensuring fairness in the resolution of local rivalries.

Along the way, there were many incidents, some intense and highly professional. On the other hand, many had a surreal quality and would be hard to believe if one had not lived through them. One of each follows.

∞   ∞   ∞

It was about 6.30 pm, and I was sitting in Ashton's pub in Clonskeagh with another member of the board that licensed many of the hospital's activities. We were discussing the agenda of a special board meeting which was convened to consider if the hospital could be allowed to continue. There was a strong case for not renewing the licence which was due to expire at the end of the week. However, were this to happen, the hospital would not be able to function, and would have to cease treatments for many cancer patients.

At minimum, this would cause major disruption. We understood that Michael Noonan (then Minister for Health) and his officials (already under pressure from the blood scandals) were camped out in Mulligan's Pub in Poolbeg Street just opposite the then headquarters of the Department of Health. They were waiting for the decision of the licensing board, and apparently had a press release prepared in case the news was bad.

The board meeting was long, intense and difficult. The chairman (a medical doctor) and the CEO (a lifelong civil servant) were both implacably opposed to not renewing the licence. However, some members, supported by the board's officials, were less than happy with the hospital and felt the *status quo* could not be allowed to stand. Thus, the board was torn between the disruption that would follow failure to renew the licence and prolonging the existing arrangements which were corrosive to safety and the quality of the hospital's services.

After hours of debate a decision was reached. The hospital's licence would be renewed, but not for the two-year period that was the norm. Instead, it would be renewed for periods of a week at a time. In addition, the hospital would be inspected weekly, initially by an inspector from outside the state. Some treatments would not be allowed until the arrangements for them improved. These restrictions would continue until the situation was turned around or it was demonstrated to be intractable, in which case the hospital would have to close.

So, the board meeting ended, not with a bang, but with considerably more than a whimper. While nobody was happy, the situation was materially changed, and an opportunity had been created to put things right without major disruption. Going into the meeting I had felt that the only solution that would result in real reform was closure. Afterwards, I was relieved to have made the case trenchantly, but was surprised to be glad not to have won the day. The following months brought an endless round of initiatives, meetings and attempts to foster change and consensus. Often the devil was in the detail: we could easily agree on the general objectives, but how to deliver them was another matter. Day-by-day progress was made, and we patched up the leaking ship while trying to keep it afloat. An almost surreal example of this follows.

∞   ∞   ∞

I met the hospital CEO for breakfast in the Davenport Hotel behind Trinity. Originally, it had been arranged for Take Five, a nearby student cafe, which seemed convenient. However, a chance conversation raised an alert. Apparently, the CEO took dining invitations seriously and expected the best. So a quick change in plan averted a near miss, and saw us in the Davenport. We were considering a list of things that needed to be done, which included the possibility of moving one of the hospital schools to college. However, he announced:

'Top of the list this week must be that crazy dispensing room we have for radioactive materials. We must fix that now; nobody could stand over it.'

'Yes, definitely needs to be done,' I responded. 'Have you approached the Department of Health for funds?'

'Of course. But the mad f-----s just ignore me. What can you do with them?'

'Have they been up to see the situation?'

'No.'

'Well, now's your chance!' I replied. 'Contact them today and tell them they need to see it, and that it needs to be attended to immediately. Suggest they arrange a visiting party with sufficient clout to act.'

His face lit up. On good days he could be manic and now there was a gleam in his eye. We quickly worked through the remainder of that day's list and, having paid the bill, I departed. Some days later, I met with him again, this time in his hospital office.

'The crowd from Health are coming up about the dispensing room,' he announced with a flourish, and the manic gleam was now unquestionable.

He bounced around the room rearranging bundles of papers, checking surfaces for dust, looking out the window and so on. The phone rang. He stared at it accusingly, allowed it to ring 12 times until it stopped, then lifted the receiver, banged it down again and shouted at the unknown caller:

'Obviously, you haven't enough to do!'

'That's great news about the visit,' I said to break the spell. 'When are they due?'

'Tomorrow morning,' he responded.

'Unfortunately, I won't be able to be here.'

'Well, it'll be okay. We'll go ahead anyway. I've a plan that'll frighten the bejaysus out of them.'

'That's good,' I responded, glad not to be part of something alarming. 'We'll probably get some action.'

I departed, hoping he would have calmed down by the time of the visit, and not really believing he would implement his plan. This is his account of what happened. He greeted the visiting party, which consisted of a group of senior architects, doctors, engineers and civil servants, in his office. After a brief orientation, they proceeded to the dispensing facility. He stopped the group just short of the door to the facility. He then made an elaborate production of advancing to the door, opening it gingerly, and rapidly withdrawing to where the group was standing. Then he explained: 'This is our problem:

84

the dispensing room for radioactivity. It is so dangerous we cannot allow you into it without protective clothing. Now that the door is open, the footprint of the risk of radiation contamination extends into the corridor. Is this clear to everybody?' He paused for confirmation from the visiting party, and they all nodded assent. He continued. 'We are giving you a rare opportunity to see what is involved. But, as I said, you cannot enter the room and the risk extends into the corridor, so this is what you must do: line up here, one behind the other. Then in turn, each of you must run quickly past the room entrance and look directly into it as you gallop past.'

And apparently, so it happened. All quite unnecessary. The hazards were real but did not need quite such a dramatic approach. But he felt it was important to make his point even if it required drama and created a narrative of danger the visitors would not forget. Subsequently, he regaled us with accounts of the incident many times. Regardless of his eccentric behaviour, the CEO was at the vanguard of trying to solve the hospital's problems, well ahead of the medical and professional staffs. But he enjoyed a sense of mischief that also made him a part of the problem.

By Christmas, a lot of progress had been made and new staff were offered, and some had accepted, leadership posts that would facilitate reform. For me, it was time to withdraw, or at least move well back from day-to-day involvement. The CEO and chairman of the board were anxious to have a small celebration to mark progress. All involved had been through a traumatic process. Hard things had been said on all sides, difficult decisions had to be implemented and, while we shared a common purpose, the interpersonal relationships involved were cool at best. Only time would deal with that. Yet, a small lunch was arranged in the boardroom for those most involved, and inevitably a few short speeches were on the agenda.

Travelling to the hospital that morning, I tried to think of a sentiment that might be appropriate. The hospital had been lurching from one unstable position to another, month after month. Now it was steadying and becoming a safe place in which patients received competent treatments. The experience, though not pleasant, was memorable, and memorable seemed a good farewell sentiment to build on. A quarter of a century later, it is still memorable. Recalling it now, I am amazed that such an intense reform was achieved through self-examination within the health service, without a single word in the public prints.

These arrangements were in place by the end of 1994 and I still have a copy of a fulsome thank-you letter from the board. But it wasn't all over yet. A few weeks later I received a summons from the courts to answer charges on inadequate control of radiation of sources at the hospital. The prosecution arose from finding unsecured radioactive sources when premises that had been in the care of the hospital were put up for sale. The case proceeded, but the CEO feared for his own fate if the case went against the hospital. He retained the best and brightest barrister in the state, the late Adrian Hardiman, who ran rings around the less well-prepared prosecuting counsel. The case was lost although a point was made.

Thereafter, the situation improved greatly with major public investment in new buildings, equipment, and staff. But confidence in public provision of many of the services involved had eroded considerably. In consequence, there was a rapid commitment to planning related services in the new private hospitals that were then an emerging feature of the health service throughout the state. More recently, they also had a prominent role in underwriting the response to the Covid-19 pandemic.

And this was still not the end of the story. In 2018 a bricked-up house in a south side Dublin suburb was offered for sale. It had been owned by a somewhat eccentric former staff member of the hospital and it fell into disrepair due to his intense involvement with his life's work. The garage door did not fit well and needed to be propped closed. He achieved this by parking his car in perpetuity wedging the door shut. The garden became overgrown, and a tree fell on the house.

After he became unwell and went into care, the council ordered the house to be bricked up. As the sales campaign progressed, some unease emerged as it was known that our eccentric alumnus used to bring his work home and containers for transporting radiation sources were found in the house. Indeed, the attic space was filled with large polystyrene boxes labelled with attention-demanding radiation hazard warnings. These were the packing material in which weekly deliveries were made to the hospital. Our eccentric hero had purloined them as attic insulation without removing the hazard notices. Eventually, the premises were formally assessed by inspectors and certified to be clear of radiation hazards, and there has been no further sighting of interesting artefacts from the hospital since.

Chapter Five

But What about the Physics...?!

Know then thyself, presume not God to scan,
The proper study of mankind is Man.
– Alexander Pope

For the most part, quantum theory has been of
little practical value in my life.
– Jenny Diski

As these Tales progressed, I often brought them to the Trinity Retirement Association writing group. The reactions were generally encouraging and helped improve them. I also occasionally asked friends or colleagues to read chapters they might find interesting. One reader disturbed me with this reaction:

'But what about the physics?' she asked.

'What about it?' I responded.

'You haven't written anything about it. And it's supposed to be important to you.'

'I haven't written about it because people are seldom interested in physics. It's not exactly a winning dinner party topic,' I countered.

'It is interesting,' she responded. 'People like Brian Cox's programmes on BBC 4. They're about the universe and physics and so on; and it's not just because he's good looking.'

'Not sure the female physicists in St James's Hospital would agree with you. In fact, at one point, three smart, classy, thirty-something women physicists would regale us with descriptions of the professions they adopted for a night on the town, including, among others, masseuse! For them physics was a no-no in terms of capturing male interest, in that context at least.'

'Well,' she responded. 'Maybe they're right about the nightclub scene, not the most winning introductory line. But they're wrong in general. I'm interested. How do you make the religion stuff and the physics hang together?'

'That's not a problem,' I said.

'That's the reason you should write about it.'

That stopped me dead. She was right, and it was something I had been avoiding. The topic would have to be excavated, and who knows what might be lurking when some of the larger boulders were moved. Of course, Brian Cox's programmes were enjoyable and some of them were even inspiring. He gathered up much of physics and used it to shine a light on the enigma of existence. They also induced an unspoilt emotion that took me back to childhood. What follows is the tale of this emotion, which was lurking under the first stone lifted and maybe is why it took so long to risk looking. The trajectory of this feeling continued from childhood into adult life (see Chapter Two).

In the 1950s, an American exhibition called Atoms for Peace visited Dublin. It followed a speech made at the United

Nations by US President Eisenhower, in which he proposed establishing an organisation to address the risks and hopes of a nuclear future. The travelling exhibition and a related programme supplied information and demonstrations to schools, hospitals and research institutions around the world. Also, work began on forming the Vienna-based International Atomic Energy Agency (IAEA), a member of the UN family. Its mission was to promote peaceful use of nuclear energy and inhibit its military applications. The exhibition and talk about peaceful applications of science were inspiring. Over half a century later, I marvel at how innocent we were, and at the randomness of the things that shape our lives. Without the Atoms for Peace exhibition, my life's trajectory would not have included a physics career that resulted in being recruited by the IAEA over half a century later (Chapters Eight and Nine). Even more striking, the link did not become apparent until after I started work in Vienna.

But something else also happened around the time of the exhibition. My much-loved grandfather died, and I was deemed old enough to help Granny rearrange her house. There was much to learn about furniture, painting, hanging wallpaper, laying carpets and becoming a general purpose, go-to handy-boy. Also, Granny's was a quiet house with some books, a big encyclopaedia and private places to read. This was a wonderful indulgence for a person normally in a house filled with four wild younger brothers and their friends. I took to investigating the books, reading them while lying on the floor of Granny's back dining room. The encyclopaedia had astronomy pictures but the real treat, silently awaiting discovery, was a few astronomy books by Sir James Jeans, a popular science writer of the time. So it was there, lying on the floor reading and absorbing every detail, that a definitive interest in science took up residence in my life. It never left, though eventually the credibility of some of the more grandiose claims of astronomy leave me cold.

All of this was percolating away but didn't find much outlet in the O'Connell's Christian Brother's Schools, even when the transition to secondary and long trousers came along (Chapter Seven). At the tea table at home, my father would now and then pose the question:

'Now boys, who is going to tell me what you will do when you grow up?'

This normally provoked a chorus of answers like 'engine driver', 'shopkeeper' and so on, depending on what was in the air at the time. After the Atoms for Peace exhibition, my feeling was that the question demanded a more serious answer, and one evening I grandly announced:

'I'm going to be an atomic scientist.'

Whatever that was, it silenced the table, and I knew little of what it would take to become one. But I could see it had taken my father's interest. He was wise enough not to pursue the matter, which could have collapsed into an episode of hilarity among the siblings. A moment many years later required similar discretion, when my daughter responded to the same question that she intended to become a tightrope walker.

Despite diversions and deviations, a sense of awe persisted through secondary school and was eventually a dominant consideration in determining a career choice. Its focus moved around and was divided between physics in its various forms, and the religious (Chapter Two). Both shared a kind of star quality in my mind, but both were also often neglected. However, the interest was easily rekindled when one or other re-emerged, like the relationship with a friend that has been absent for a while. What had they in common? It is difficult to say, but as well as being awesome, both seemed to promise access to something that was solid and could be verified: a form of truth? At the time this was an important if naïve feeling.

The late teens were a restless time and about two years after leaving school this became troublesome and couldn't be ignored any more. My parents had encouraged me to consider options like the civil service and the banks. Both had qualifying exams that weren't challenging, but to me neither seemed worth the trouble. Likewise, following in my father's footsteps, I had a brief flirtation with electronic engineering, which though interesting and technically demanding had not yet become 'awesome'. By default, the lack of inspiration in what society demanded or offered brought religion back into the picture, and the form it took on this occasion was an attraction to Franciscan life (Chapter Two). It offered a real outlet for the sense of awe that had been present for so long. It also respected nature, which was attractive to a young person at a time when Rachel Carson's *Silent Spring* first appeared. Although the physics was also still there, it was parked unobtrusively.

The first year with the Franciscans was devoted to the practicalities of a spiritual life, and we saw little of theology or academic studies. The lifestyle sustained a sense of awe – there was much of liturgy, two meditation sessions each day and various other practices. In addition, we had some formal instruction on aspects of the spiritual life, but it did not amount to much. While it was embedded in teachings from fathers of the church and the founders of the Franciscan tradition, it took little account of new knowledge in psychology and the humanities which had much to offer. We emerged from this year having encountered Rudolf Otto's sense of the numinous, the *mysterium tremendum et fascinans*. And bright-eyed, we were dispatched to Galway to do a degree. There, we confronted the practicality of choosing a subject and starting serious study. We were jolted from stargazing and the transcendent to a very different reality.

The Franciscans were relaxed about the subjects you took for a first degree. Eventually, everyone studying for the priesthood with them would complete at least two degrees, one in philosophy (normally in Galway or in Louvain for those of a scholarly disposition) and one in theology (always in Rome). However, those with a capacity to do so were encouraged to first study for degrees in secular subjects, and about half did so, usually in the arts or humanities. A smaller proportion opted for one of the sciences and of those a few did mathematics or physics. At that time, nobody opted for engineering, though a few did agricultural science, which could be regarded as a type of engineering.

Having such options open was a surprise, and quickly took on the aspect of manna from heaven. Suddenly, quantum physics and cosmology were back on the agenda. In addition, as others pointed out, the registration queues in the university for mathematics and physics were much shorter than those for arts subjects. It is now hard to believe that the queue for the classics and Latin was still longer than those for any of the sciences. It was such a different world, before the points system, before free secondary education, and participation was still relatively low and elitist. So, in October 1964 I registered for a physics degree in Galway and began an exploration of one of the most exciting sciences before its reputation was soiled by many transgressions, including the literal and figurative fallout from the first nuclear bombs. Side by side with this was exploration of the spiritual life, living in community with 60 to 100 others engaged in study of the humanities and languages. It was like being in a university in the old-fashioned sense, where a great diversity of knowledge existed and was cherished under one roof.

Less than four years later, we had lived through exciting times, Vatican II had come and gone, both of the Kennedy brothers had been assassinated, free secondary education was established, the 1968 student revolution was in full swing, and civil rights movements were underway in Northern Ireland and throughout the world. And I had started to doubt both science and God ...

Doubt initially felt like unbelief, particularly in the context of being a Franciscan. Later, doubt and uncertainty normalised and a kind of unknowing became part of life. But, as a young Franciscan, it felt like negation of something central. Leaving was an option, and I was assured of a welcome at home. The feeling gradually built up and was deeply troubling. While I did not want to leave, staying became difficult to live with, and the situation could not be resolved.

Eventually, I approached an elderly priest, let's call him 'Father Walter', hoping for advice and clarity. He lived in the Franciscan student house in Galway and was more of an academic/philosopher than a priest/theologian. For example, I have no memory of him saying mass. His was a quiet and detached life with few indulgences, except for a weakness for western films and smoking a pipe. He held a senior appointment in the university, and I had surreptitiously slipped into some of his lectures which were excellent. He had a good understanding of the history and philosophy of science and had published a book on the topic.

I hadn't been in his room prior to this, and so entered it with some trepidation. It was a scholar's room, books and papers scattered about the place in a kind of orderly chaos. He was welcoming and had a natural unhurried presence that made it easy to chat without getting to the point. However, I eventually threw caution to the wind and spat out the big worry:

'Was it possible, in good conscience, to continue the practices of living a religious life – participating at mass and communion every day, meditation, the Divine Office and so on – while at the same time having real doubts about the God that was supposed to guide the whole enterprise?' And after a pause, I continued: 'After all, was this not a negation of the life and most of its practices? An insult to it?'

I had been brought up in the 1950s when we were taught *apologetics* in secondary school. It was a rigorous philosophical and theological system justifying precise statements of the beliefs we were expected to hold. This, like the classics, encouraged critical thinking, but only allowed for the official conclusion. Departing from that was viewed as a worthwhile kind of sin, and not just a relatively tolerable sexual misdemeanour, about which some people were becoming more relaxed. But the Second Vatican Council, which was in progress, seemed to have different priorities.

Father Walter was unperturbed. There were no thunderbolts. The atmosphere in the room remained quiet and welcoming. The spring sunshine outside the window absorbed his attention. After a pause, he enquired if I had a sense of where the doubts might be coming from. I felt that the years of physics were taking their toll, and even though they had their own uncertainties, they demanded a habit of mind that seemed to challenge religion. He didn't contradict this but also didn't affirm it. But he felt my problem might be a consequence of taking scholarship seriously. He continued that with any other subject the outcome could have been similar. This surprised me and turned the matter on its head. Einstein is reported to have remarked that 'the serious research scholar … is the only true religious person (today).'

The conversation went on for a long time. He eventually intimated (advice would be too strong a word) that there was no reason to leave that he could see. What was going on was growth and should be welcomed rather than be resisted. With more experience, honesty would come to a resolution consistent with the truth (whatever that is) and I was being honest. In the meantime, he suggested, it was reasonable to continue fully in the practices of the house and not to be worried about doing so. His door was open should I wish to talk with him again.

What a relief – what a burden lifted. My troubled state of mind was normalised, and he did so without recourse to facile solutions that would not have been helpful (for example, suggesting praying about it). Leaving his room was like, to misquote Seamus Heaney, 'walking on air, against my better judgment' (Chapter Three). The following months were much easier – there was still a problem – but guilt or impropriety were no longer part of it.

This somewhat experimental state lasted less than a year, during which time it resolved itself decisively and without stress in favour of leaving. Uncertainty continued, it distinguished itself from doubt, and both gained a foothold in physics over and above their official place. This was the relatively silent beginning of an adult form of faith, which is just as necessary to science as it is to religion. They gradually became an unobtrusive background to the 'real' world and were reinforced by the flawed understanding of sexuality and the inability to embrace new knowledge that persisted in the churches. Side by side with this was a growing unease with science and its public/political role, particularly in respect of the arms race and nuclear fallout in the 1960s. In 1968, I left the Franciscans, grateful for a wonderful experience, and decided to give science a full-on try.

∞ ∞ ∞

I loved the pure mathematical form in which the understanding of nature is expressed in physics, particularly the big beasts like Schrödinger's and Dirac's Quantum Mechanics for the atomic and subatomic worlds, and Einstein's Relativity for the grand cosmic scale. These fascinated once one was at ease with the (mathematical) language that carried them. They have an elegance, coherence and completeness not encountered in other parts of life. But they also had their flaws.

There were other less grand, less classy, areas of physics that were nonetheless satisfying. These included, for example, a classical theory of gasses (the kinetic theory of gasses), the older Newtonian mechanics, the physics of solids and some parts of thermodynamics. The latter included the celebrated Second Law of Thermodynamics, which C.P. Snow made the benchmark for scientific illiteracy in his celebrated 1970s book *The Two Cultures*.

But there were less salubrious parts of physics that did not share the glamour of quasi-mystical theories. These were to be found in the empirical aspects of heat, temperature, sound, elasticity, fluid flow, optics and some parts of nuclear science. They often seemed a bit clunky in terms of their relationship with the grand vision and the big theories. Though grounded in observation, and of great practical importance, they are second-class citizens. So, science hosts an almost inexplicable hierarchical class structure at its heart.

Most aspects of physics find applications that crop up in everything from the internet to printers, from double glazing to the texture of food products, and from mobile phone cameras to the efficacy of airbrakes. The applications are omnipresent, much more so than in the 1960s when they were less visible. In addition, while the consequences of the inherent uncertainties of physics sustained a somewhat tarnished sense of awe, the existence of the uncertainty itself eventually becomes its most awe-inspiring feature. Despite the positives, I had instinctive reservations about the thrust of applied physics. Therefore, my focus moved towards areas with a real possibility of being useful that avoided any connection with the defence industry. This quickly led to medical physics, and a half century of fascination followed.

In science, the arc of sustainable interest waxed and waned and what inspired awe was a moveable feast. For example, the grand scale of astronomical infinity held court for a long time, but its star eventually declined, partly through being replaced by the busyness and business of family and professional life. The excesses of its brasher advocates like Fred Hoyle in the 1970s, and later Stephen Hawkins, helped undermine it. Both claimed too much for astronomy and scientific cosmology; they abandoned physics for an authoritative form of *meta*-physics that any self-respecting archbishop would eschew. Excessive extrapolation in astronomy and particle physics became almost cartoon-like.

Big physics, particularly the nuclear variety, and its successor big sciences (including molecular biology and genomics) dominate for a time, but eventually disappoint, partly through overpromising and especially through their unforeseen consequences. They often function without a sense of ethics or history, and the careerists in academic departments are full partners to the repeated failures of this short-sighted approach. At the time of writing, there are movements to counter these excesses.

The background noise of funding and research contracts in big science distracts from the engagement with nature and data that is a must for the scientist. When contact with reality is direct, experiential and honest, it will surprise from time to time. From this the sense of awe may emerge, come home, assert itself, exercise its compelling magic, and settle in the smaller infinity within us. It is similar whether it attaches to the vastness and impenetrability of the cosmos or drawing a simple, interpretative graph. It arises from the ultimate, inscrutable unknowability of the world, as did whatever intrigued and inspired during Archbishop Fogarty's Sunday liturgies in the 1950s cathedral in Ennis (Chapter Two). The mystique persists today, but the balance between the intellectual and the emotional has changed. Complete explanations are not expected, and inherent embedded uncertainties now reside in many disciplines. When certainty occasionally tries to reassert itself, it is short-lived, except among some theologians.

The transition from certainty eventually settled into a sense that whatever the world is about is beyond anything I can hope to know and make sense of. The journey to this point was sometimes uncomfortable but has, for now, settled in a peaceful place. Two quotes often come to mind in this context. The first, from John Banville, is at the front of his novel *Shroud*:

> *We set up a word at the point at which our ignorance begins, at which we can see no further ... (the words) are perhaps the horizon of our knowledge, but not truths.*

I take comfort in Banville's clever sentence when it is applied to words like God. It is a word used so often to protect us from how little we really know. On a different note, the South African President de Klerk is reported to have said:

> *I believe in God. But I don't know if he exists. Nor do I know if there is more than one.*

Likewise, Mary Warnock, who did ground-breaking work on ethics for education and for the human genome project, identified as an atheist *and* a devout Anglican. Here the word atheist is nuanced, just as the word God would need to be, if it was inserted into Banville's sentence.

So, if there is something beyond He, She or It is mysterious beyond anything my imagination can relate to. I don't bother He, She or It with prayers for this that or the other. But being present to whoever or whatever might be there does seem important. That is *faith* to me, and there are moments when the veil lifts a little, suggesting a benign presence. Which gives some *hope* that it is so, despite strong evidence to the contrary in man's actions and nature's capacity for arbitrary destruction. I try to live with respect for creation and those with whom the planet, our city, our workplaces, and our homes are shared. In practice, this feels like *charity*, the Golden Rule. And liturgy still appeals, even though its texts leave me, like Michael Harding, perplexed but not in the least worried about it. After all, Brian Friel pointed out in his great work *Translations* that 'confusion is not a dishonourable state'.

Part of the journey of middle life and later lay with realising that the quest for perfection is not just unreasonable, but there is something fascist about it, a position championed by artist Sean Scully. Indeed, it became clear that imperfection is not just the way things are, but it is an essential part of life. It makes many things attractive and can be the consequence of an untidy, disruptive creative impulse. It is the difference between cold beauty and being hot. Or 'the happy fault' of Adam's sin celebrated in the great Easter hymn, *Exultet* (*O Felix Culpa*). A minor example from my own experience was mitching from school. I used to feel this was wrong, but in reality it is a refreshing and energising practice that continues (if in a different form) even to the present day (Chapter Seven).

As a young man, I read everything that came my way, from thrillers to Dostoyevsky and *Dr Zhivago*. These had some impact at the time and leave something of a glow, but they were not transformative in the way some later reading was. For example, both Graham Greene's and C.P. Snow's novels were part of the background to my twenties/thirties and were very influential. Greene gave a rich account of the comforts and the burdens of Catholicism as it was then, and both recognised and accepted the flawed nature of the world as we find it. Both writers were true to experience, and often challenged conventional thinking.

C.P. Snow's novels provided an insider account of what it was like to be a practicing scientist. Until then most science writing was at the gee-whizz, absent-minded professor level or science fiction. I was lucky enough to start with *The Masters*, a novel of college life in Cambridge; it also described with empathy aspects of professional and academic life in England which until then had remained outside the literary canon.

Snow's novels provide a sweeping narrative of twentieth century professional life, including science, and are unrivalled in their descriptions of what drives the players involved. Snow captures the court politics of scientists and public servants and their manoeuvring in the corridors of power (a phrase we owe to him). He fell foul of the high priests of literary criticism, who replaced archbishops as arbiters of all that is good and true for a while. But that does not take from his work. After all, Terry Eagleton, the high priest of the species, declared critical theory to be dead and himself to be an evolutionary dead end. Snow's accounts of attempts to produce a nuclear device in England are as good as it gets. He foreshadowed what has become a central problem in science when careerism and fraud sacrifice the truth and put the whole edifice at risk, something also addressed by Ian McEwan in his novel *Solar*.

Later, in middle life, reading that favoured a sense of mystery occasionally came along, though it was seldom planned. This sense flies under the radar, it subtly creates its own opportunities and refuses to be sidelined indefinitely. Many examples occurred, often involving casually reading novels or later poetry, ostensibly for entertainment. But novels and poems not only entertain – they sneak up on you, inform and disrupt. Their efficiency as carriers of truth is alarming.

They can be transformative, and when we allow them, they exercise this magic without much conscious intervention.

By the 1990s I recognised the strength of these influences, and perhaps an example won't go amiss. Over time, I consumed the Irish canon of English prose fiction and had loved it well, but gradually moved away, tiring of its relentless misery. A psychologist friend recommended Robertson Davies's novel *Rebel Angels*. Davies, a Canadian, wrote wonderful novels of academic and professional life in the arts, journalism, the theatre and so on. These have sweeping narratives and are garnished with a Jungian understanding of people and events. Unlike many modern writers Davies also had a deep, questioning religious sensibility.

Rebel Angels is a novel of life in a long-established university. It felt like the Oxbridge Universities or Trinity College Dublin. There were, for example, the excellent committed academics sidelined into becoming good citizens of the university and having regrets about neglecting their own research and scholarship. There was also a menacing sense of evil lurking in the undergrowth, and its capacity to generate support for its agenda in a college community not alert to it.

What a treat his novels were. They consolidated a move to literature, including poetry, as the strongest influences in my spiritual life, something that I didn't articulate for a while, but it was no less real for that. The inner lives of the main protagonists, both good and evil, were visible. His dozen or so unforgettable novels had characters with much to say about life, the universe and everything, and how we fit into it. I was captivated and read and re-read his work, often saving it up for times of isolation. Davies was given an Honorary Degree by Trinity College in 1990. I would like to have been at the ceremony but had to settle for the next best thing: being away reading his work (Chapter Eight). In *The Cornish Trilogy*, he puts the following in the mouth of a 23-year-old female graduate student of the late 1970s:

> *Rabelais was gloriously learned because learning amused him, and ... that is learning's best justification. Not the only one, but the best. It is not that I wanted to know a great deal, in order to acquire what is called expertise, and which enables one to become an expert-tease ... I hoped for bigger fish. I wanted nothing less than wisdom. In a modern university if you ask for knowledge they will provide it in almost any form ... But if you ask for wisdom ... God save us all! What a show of modesty, what disclaimers from the men and women from whose eyes intelligence shines forth like a lighthouse. ... Intelligence, yes, but of Wisdom not so much as the gleam of a single candle. ... And Paracelsus said: The striving for wisdom is the second paradise of the world.*

There were many other inspiring novelists, far too numerous to discuss, and I will mention only two: Haruki Murakami and Kazuo Ishiguro. The latter creates slow, absorbing narratives, gentle in their detail but horrifying and disturbing in their conclusion, such as Booker Prize winner *The Remains of the Day*. Murakami, on the other hand, writes extraordinary novels with a surreal dimension that respects the fluidity of our perceptions of reality and both charm and excite with their recognition of possibilities outside of the ordinary.

When the new millennium dawned, I was in my mid-fifties, and the folly of being eternally busy could no longer be ignored. A newly cultivated life skill, that is, successfully resigning from committees helped (Chapter Seven). The main component of this skill was to become slightly more cranky and demanding at meetings. These allowed resignations to go ahead and did away with pressures to stay on. Studious attention to Machiavelli's small 'p' court politics, which define life in universities and hospitals, helped. There are unexpected consequences of resignations, notably something better often comes along that might not otherwise have happened. Disengaging provided growth opportunities and allowed one time to exist. With practice, the habit matured, and soon the big one beckoned: early retirement in 2002 at age 58. The starting date for this new life was October 4, the feast day of St Francis of Assisi. I happily joined the ranks of those who *were gone but not yet forgotten*, as opposed to those who were *forgotten but not gone!* Now, there were numerous things to explore in the arts, humanities and religion, but I had no idea where to start.

There was much talk then of bioethics, particularly in relation to the human genome and genetic engineering. The field looked exciting, did not seem to be oversubscribed, and the research was potentially the most dangerous on the planet. Over the weeks and months before retirement I met people, including the Head of Ethics at the Milltown Institute, a Jesuit who had moved out of the Jesuit house downtown into a Ballymun flat. This gave him a new perspective on the rights and wrongs in human transactions. While he could see that I might find the area interesting, he was not encouraging, and that made me pause. He was wise, and I started to wonder if the ethics *per se* would be awe inspiring. The molecular research was, but the ethics?

A friend informed me of an open day at The Milltown Institute in 2002. I vividly remember walking up its tree-lined avenue in early autumn. It had something of the seclusion and reflective atmosphere of the Franciscan Student House of a half century earlier. A middle-aged lady in the entrance hall introduced herself. We chatted about this and that, eventually homing in on whatever had drawn me to the open day, and I mentioned retirement and bioethics. She was not very interested and enquired about things outside professional life. We then discussed literature, novels, poetry, the Merriman Summer School and music and dancing. She was more interested, the conversation grew, and we chatted about spirituality, the mystics, psychology, the visual arts and cinema and a sense of awe.

She explained they had an MA programme that addressed personal spirituality, but undergraduate theology was a required entry qualification. I had no theology but had often been on the other side of the formalities for entry to courses and was able to talk my way in. And so, with heartfelt thanks to this person and many others in Milltown, a wonderful journey started through anthropology of religions, contemporary culture, the arts, psychology, literature and much more. I found a place where scholarship and religious experience sat together easily with Yeats and Wilde – the pilgrim soul finding inspiration not only in the stars, but also in turning to the smaller infinity within. By year two, I sometimes sensed a barely discernible echo of Teilhard de Chardin's remarkable description of his inner life:

> *And so for the first time in my life ... I took the lamp and, leaving the zone of everyday occupations and relationships where everything seems clear, I went down into my inmost self, to the deep abyss whence I feel dimly that my power of action emanates. But as I moved further and further away from the conventional certainties by which social life is superficially illuminated, I became aware that I was losing contact with myself. ... And when I had to stop*

my exploration because the path faded from beneath my steps, I found a bottomless abyss at my feet, and out of it came – arising I know not from where – the current which I dare to call my life.

That, from the priest-scientist, is about as awe inspiring as it gets, even at a time when neurophysics and the neurosciences have much to tell us about meditative and mystical states.

Interlude

Chapter Six

And Thanks are Due to ...

*Ar scáth a chéile a mhaireann na
daoine. (People live in each other's
shadow/shelter).*

– An Irish proverb quoted by
President Michael D Higgins

*This city weaves itself so intimately
it is hard to see, despite the tenacity
of the river.... I am as much at home
here as I will ever be.*

– Sinead Morrissey

We all owe much to those who have nourished and sheltered us during our formative years. Without realising it, we become a reincarnation of at least some of the qualities they lived out in front of us. In my case, the strong influences included parents, grandparents, siblings, spouse, family and friends, acquaintances, professional colleagues and both the places I lived in as well as the institutions I became part of. To all I offer thanks but here will only write specifically about my parents and grandparents, all of whom have passed on, and will also touch on a few places lived in. I will not write about my siblings or my own family, except occasionally in passing. All are alive at the time of writing and there is nothing in the *Tales* that requires their privacy be disturbed.

Legacy of a quiet man

Some memories of my father are sufficient in themselves and easy to be with. Others do not sit quietly and most of my memories of him are of this type. They are never unpleasant, but they quickly ignite a train of thought on how difficult it is to have a clear view of what he was about or where he was going. A few rambling speculative memories shrouded in uncertainty are recalled here, and hopefully they lend some substance to an otherwise shadowy impression.

First a few matters of fact. He was born in Dunboyne, County Meath on December 4, 1916, and was known as JJ, Seamus or Jim. He was the oldest of three children, received a scholarship from Dublin County Council on the strength of which he attended O'Connell Schools, and obtained an honours Leaving Certificate. Seventy-three years, five months and about twenty-five days after he was born, I dropped into the family home in Clontarf on a weekday morning. He was in the front garden, in an old pullover and well-worn gardening trousers. He struck me as being happy, and in an exceptional way was at peace with himself and the world. A few days later, at roughly the same time, I received the phone call saying he was dead. This final memory, and what I felt was discernible of his state of mind in the last days of May 1990, is uplifting. If his experience of serious heart disease was anything like mine (and I have reason to believe it was) he may well have been aware that he was at high risk at the time.

During his life he had been a clerical student briefly, and worked in a few administrative jobs, also briefly. Thereafter he self-studied, becoming a ship's radio officer, and started a life-long love of boats and the sea. Later he became an electrical engineer specialising in radar and telecommunications, and eventually joined the civil service, where his work had a large international component. He married Nancy in 1942, and they had six children, four of whom still survive at the time of writing. From age about 40 he battled with cardiovascular disease in various forms, and steadfastly refused to become an invalid until the day he died.

Can anything be inferred from the three names he was known by? It is by no means unusual to be known by more than one name. Two is common, but three is probably exceptional. Perhaps they give a clue to different faces he showed to the world. His mother Rose and sister May always referred to him as JJ. The initials did not then have the corporate ring they later acquired. It was also common then to use other initials, PJ being the most frequent. His wife Nancy always called him Seamus. This was never explained at home. However, it is probable that he was introduced to her as JJ; they most likely met through his sister when she and Nancy worked in the Land Commission. It is also conceivable that he took steps to move away from JJ and preferred Seamus: this was the name he used on many notebooks dating from the 1930s up to the 1950s. Perhaps not unconnected, he had a low-key republican leaning and consistently patronised the *Irish Press* for as long as it was available. I suspect that he also favoured it because of its higher level of factual reportage. The other papers relied more heavily on opinion pieces and columnists, which he did not have much time for.

He was dutiful regarding wife and family and developed an unusual lifestyle that was possibly necessary for the equilibrium he generally displayed. I can only recall two occasions when anger broke through, and at his funeral many observed that it was difficult to recall any occasions when he had spoken ill of somebody. This is in accord with my own memories. A story, which he enjoyed telling, provides his outer boundary for personal criticism. Following the 1973 general election Conor Cruise O'Brien (Labour Party, and former United Nations diplomat) was appointed Minister of Posts and Telegraph. In effect, this meant that the Cruiser (as the Minister was known) became Dad's boss. Dad, an engineer, was asked to investigate the TV in the Minister's office, which was regularly but intermittently on the blink. He quickly diagnosed the problem: it seems that there was a potted plant on top of the TV set and the Minister regularly watered it. And we all know that water and electricity don't mix well. The telling implied that the sophisticated minister lacked common sense; many would agree.

∞   ∞   ∞

His hobbies included amateur radio, astronomy, sailing, boatbuilding and making or repairing almost anything. Many of these activities were relatively solitary and some involved the occasional participation of a small group of longstanding friends. But he introduced most of us as children to at least some of these, so all of us acquired enduring interests or skills without realising it, from watching him in action or participating in his projects. In due course, some of his grandchildren also benefited from exposure to these interests. So now, among his children and grandchildren, there are several amateur radio enthusiasts, several sailors, numerous amateur astronomers and many with excellent DIY skills. But no football team.

Sea voyages, foreign business travel and trips to his grand-parents' small farm in Derryoghill, County Longford, pro-vided abundant opportunities for a solitude that he needed. I never sensed that he was unhappy about the extent of his 'duty-travel' and the separation it brought. The amount of it was unusual. Even in the 1950s, it could be months on end. It was possibly nourishing for him and probably sustained his character. In the same way that other people need company or are gregarious, he needed space and a liberal dose of quiet separation. Although modern psychology might be inclined to 'correct' this, it is a Malone family trait. The McGonagles (paternal grandmother), and the O'Keeffes (my mother's fam-ily) were polar opposites, gregarious and extrovert, as was my dad's brother Willie.

The tendency to solitude left him with a strong sense of self; he did not crave or need approval, validation or atten-tion. It is fair to say that most of my siblings inherited some of this sense of self, even though it was never explicitly spoken of. He left plenty of room and freedom of action that many others did not have at the time we grew up. This was clearest in unspoken example, but also in the lack of interference or forensic screening of the people we befriended and brought home. All were welcomed and we were allowed get on with whatever the agenda of the day was. Openness of this type was less common than we recognised. He possibly felt interference or guidance was less likely to be productive than example.

He was not an overtly religious person but fell in with the pattern of Sunday mass attendance, possibly out of loyalty to Nancy. But there was a mysterious, quasi-mystical quality to him that nudges me to wonder what, if anything, moved him toward the transcendent or the possibility of there being something beyond. His hobbies were generally rooted in the practical and empirical, and he had little time for the aesthetic if it wasn't also functional. I recall his views on Dublin's Georgian buildings and how unsuitable they were as offices, probably based on years of working in a splendid Georgian house on Harcourt Street (now Conradh na Gaeilge). Notwithstanding the empiricism, it would also be easy to say his head was in the clouds, with the astronomy, the ongoing contact with distant places as a radio ham/sailor, and most of all in the sense of perfection, and new beginnings, that he often brought to his projects. He also enjoyed opera and the cinema. In the monochrome world of Ireland in the 1950s, I suspect they 'took him to the other side'. He patronised them at home and abroad. My memory is that he and my mother went to the cinema most Monday evenings and that this persisted well into the TV age.

His sense of the empirical is captured in this entry from one of the numerous notebooks he left behind. It is from the late 1940s and relates to his work as a communications engineer near what would eventually become Shannon Airport:

> As there is no aircraft up at the moment, I have time to write a few lines. I will describe this hut. It is 10' x 10' approximately. I would estimate that it is also about 10' high. The radio equipment consists of a Marconi short-wave direction-finding receiver. It is mounted on a large bench, like a shop counter which extends about three quarters of the way across the room. At the moment the other furnishings of the hut amount to the following: an electric clock, a press, a water filter, two buckets, two fire extinguishers, a coat hanger, a sweeping brush, three chairs & two blankets. Heat is provided by a tubular heating arrangement which is very inadequate in winter. This explains the necessity for the blankets. The press contains some spares for the receiver, also the necessary equipment for making and drinking tea. The hut is situated on a large

*flat area of reclaimed land, well below high tide level. It is
connected to B hut (the main building at Ballygireen), by
a path about half a mile long. The building is fully exposed
to the elements & during a gale at night it is easy to imagine oneself back at sea again.*

His life had an otherworldly quality and suggests a real,
if not clearly articulated, connection with the transcendent.
The Ireland (and indeed the western world) of the time did
not put much value on a language for such experience. I recall his response to a visit from the Chaplain during one of his
stays in the Mater Hospital. The priest enquired if he would
like anything, such as confession or communion. He replied,
in a courteous way, that he would like communion but didn't
go to confession. At the time this would have been seriously unorthodox, but he didn't seem to feel a need to explain.
Likewise, I remember his attending a funeral in a Protestant
church, which wasn't done at the time, and was the subject
of conversation among family and neighbours. But he did
not make an issue of it and didn't seem to need to comment
on or justify it. Such things have ceased to be of note today
but, at the time, they were far from trivial. His approach was
a clear lesson in having your own mind, much clearer than
being told it was important. The accumulation of incidents
like these probably had more influence on us as children than
we acknowledged at the time.

I wrote an early version of this account during a stay at
the Hotel des Alpes in Geneva, almost 20 years after his 1990
death. I was on an assignment to the World Health Organiza-
tion, and felt I was walking in his footsteps. During much of
his professional life, he spent months in Geneva every year,

working as the Irish representative to the International Tele-communications Union (one of the UN family of organisations). The hotel is small, with six floors with five rooms on each floor. There was an apartment at the top, which he liked if it was available. It is a small city centre hotel, not ostentatious, good rooms, no public spaces to speak of, modestly priced, walking distance to all the services he would be likely to want, but not in the modern cheap and cheerful mode. The railway station and trams to the UN area are at the top of the relatively short street and Lake Geneva is at the other end; there are lots of small shops and restaurants, one of which he frequented regularly: the Café de Paris. A little removed from the historic city centre, it is still 'downtown' and has the advantages and disadvantages common to such areas. Should I be surprised that I am surprised that I would pick this hotel and have often picked similar hotels when available? What's inherited is sometimes surprising because the pattern wasn't visible and hadn't yet been noticed. For a quiet man he lives on in surprising ways!

And of Nancy – a happy, gregarious woman

My mother, Nancy O'Keeffe, was born on the November 16, 1917 near Brosna village in north Kerry. She was the last of six children and came to Dublin as a young secretary in the late 1930s. Though she never lost her love of country life and her beautiful Kerry lilt, she took to the city and thrived in it. She worked in the old Land Commission offices in Upper Merrion Street where the Merrion Hotel now is. My brothers and our partners have happy memories of celebrating her 80th birthday there, and she revelled in the comparison of the stylish plush hotel with the drafty, vermin-infested offices of her working days. She had an exceptional capacity for making and retaining friends, and remained close to those from her time in the Land Commission until her final days.

Thinking of Nancy evokes many memories – so many it is difficult to choose. The selection here is mainly from her later life, which I remember best. But first a few from life in County Clare where I was born. My earliest impressions are of listening to the wireless at lunchtime. Broadcasts then were confined to the early morning, 90 minutes at lunchtime, and a few hours in the evening. The lunchtime session consisted of the news and 15-minute sponsored programmes of music and advertisements. The news tended to be about the Korean War and attempts to get peace, which Nancy always listened to. She loved music on the wireless, and it was probably the first time in her life that she had access to music every day. She joined in and sang all the popular songs of the day. I also have a clear impression of my Godmother, Maureen Malone from Oranmore, a good, enduring friend who would visit Nancy. The laughter of the two young women in the kitchen echoes down the years.

Another childhood memory is the Rosary every evening. We all knelt, using kitchen chairs as props. But my father sat. She took charge of the proceedings, first ensuring it took place and then orchestrating its content. The Rosary itself, and the Litany of the Virgin Mary (see Preface), took about 10 minutes. But she added an ever-increasing list of people and causes to be prayed for. Family members of unascertainable remoteness were prayed for if they were ill or had died. A surprising range of causes were taken up, and some of my brothers feel this was the origin of the commitment several of us made to social and international causes in the wider world. Later, when we all moved away and the family Rosary had stopped, she continued it herself. She had another practice that I discovered during her last illness, and it continued to the end. She had a bundle of memorial cards, larger than several decks of playing cards, and went through it each month. She paused to individually remember each of those she had known, both friends and family members. In her seventies she had lost her enthusiasm for looking through old photographs. However, she still enjoyed this regular reflective remembrance of all those she had known.

Another strong memory is of being off school and confined to bed in a darkened room, possibly with the mumps or measles. I vividly remember being able to hear the broadcast of the coronation of Queen Elizabeth II at Westminster Abbey in 1953. It was listened to in the kitchen with rapt attention by Nancy and a couple of female visitors. Earlier in the day, there had been a fuss to ensure the wireless would be working properly for this special event.

After we moved to Dublin, when I was approaching ten years of age, Nancy started to discuss things she was worried about with me in the evening after the others were in bed and when Dad was away. This lasted a few years until I became a stroppy teenager. I recall clearly that she was concerned that he might be thinking of moving all of us to America. She wasn't enthusiastic and had the advantage of having two sisters and other relatives who had been to the US, many of whom were happy to be back in Ireland. It never came to pass, and I think they were both happy about that, even if it meant a struggle to look after us all. I regret not having raised it again later, to see what they really felt and if their recollections accorded with mine. This was my first experience of an adult discussion, and it stays with me.

Around this time, Nancy became unwell and had to go into hospital for a hysterectomy. She confided that she was worried she might not come out alive, and was concerned at what might happen to all of us. At the time, some people felt that you only went into hospital to die, and I heard this as late as 1990 from an old neighbour in Clare. But I couldn't make the leap of imagination required to think that Mam might not be cured. She was such a presence in all our lives. After the operation she returned home very unwell and was confined to bed for a long time. But she was more at ease about the prognosis which was good. I have strong memories of cooking meals and bringing them up to her in bed. I was surprised to be told later that I helped a lot during this illness. Gradually, she got better, and gradually I advanced into the teens and the closeness of this period morphed into the conflict/confrontation of those years. Nevertheless, she encouraged each of us in whatever direction we took, and this had a strong positive impact.

Much later, she accompanied my own young family on many holidays. Inevitably, those I remember best were to the house I had in Clare. For years we went there during the Easter break and in July for the Willie Clancy Summer School, until illness eventually interrupted the pattern for her. We often had other visitors as well as the immediate family and had great walks, outings and meals. Easter lunch at the Aberdeen Arms was a great occasion. Later, the favourite was Berry Lodge, along the coast toward Quilty (see first colour insert). We were regulars there and she enjoyed the food, the company and seeing the youngsters growing up.

Willie Clancy week was special for her. She loved music and never tired of it. She went to concerts most evenings and particularly enjoyed the violin. Her favourite was watching good dancers with live music. After a few years at Willie Clancy week, she started attending dance workshops in Dublin during the winter. She was then into her seventies and continued this new hobby until her health declined.

She particularly enjoyed David Marsh, a PhD candidate working with me and a fine musician. He stayed with us most years for Willie Clancy week with his girlfriend Anne. Nancy would laugh at David disappearing in the evenings to pubs in the surrounding countryside in search of music sessions. It was often the following morning before he returned, and he sometimes feigned uncertainty as to where he had been. She loved the way he enjoyed himself and his music. Much later, he played the fiddle at her funeral, including a few gentle reels as the coffin was removed from the church. Nothing would have pleased her more.

She made lasting friendships with some of those who came and stayed during Willie Clancy Week. Perhaps the strangest involved a talented woman we will call 'Miriam'. Miriam was exceptionally successful academically and professionally, but her dress sense was, to say the least, eccentric. Back in Dublin, on impulse, Miriam decided one day that she would drop into Nancy's house for a chat. Nancy later told me that somebody had called unexpectedly. When she answered the door, she didn't immediately recognise Miriam, and assumed she was a Traveller. Nancy prepared for an exchange on that basis. However, once Miriam said something Nancy recognised her. All was well, and no damage done!

She loved theatre and concerts. Generally, she liked Irish writers, including John B. Keane, Sean O'Casey, Brendan Behan, Patrick Kavanagh and so on. She also liked Rosaleen Linehan and Des Keogh in review and would not miss an evening involving Eamon Kelly (the seanchaí) or Brendan Kennelly. Over the years we saw many of the well-known Irish music performers including De Dannan, The Chieftains, Sharon Shannon, Planxty, Christy Moore, Martin Hayes and, from another genre, the wonderful Prof Peter O'Brien, Paddy Cole et al., most of them many times. She also had an element of anarchy that I only became aware of at the National Concert Hall where bringing food or drink into the hall was strictly forbidden. But I remember noticing as she was going into the auditorium one evening that she quietly secreted her teetotaller's wine glass of lemonade under her cardigan, and who would challenge an eighty-year-old (plus) lady?

We went to special concerts each year celebrating the music of the Strauss family. These were usually part of a pre- or post-Christmas programme, elaborate affairs with an orchestra and a troupe of costumed dancers. They colourfully played and danced waltzes, marches and polkas. She loved these atmospheric, candle-lit occasions. She was a delight to bring out, always appreciative and visibly enjoyed the evening. A few years after she passed, I realised that I hadn't been at one of these concerts since her demise and that I missed them as well as her. They had become part of the year. With hindsight, it seems that elderly mothers provided many middle-aged men with an excuse to attend and enjoy these occasions; a variant on children providing adults with an excuse to go to the pantomime or the circus.

Visiting Nancy in Beaumont Hospital or at home during her last illness was a strange experience. I often felt less than enthusiastic about going to visit somebody so ill. However, she had a wonderful disposition, and I always came away feeling better after the visit. Strange that the well visitor should be buoyed up by the invalid.

At home, on two occasions in her last few months, she woke up while I was sitting with her and when she was settled and alert a conservation ensued:

'Are you okay?' she asked.

'Since they changed my tablets, I feel much better,' I replied.

'Not that. I was wondering how you're managing on your pension?'

'Oh! I don't think I've ever been better off, mortgage cleared and very few responsibilities. I get more work than I want... The money comes into my account and I don't take any notice of it, and never manage to spend much of it.'

And I went on to explain that I was a failure as a consumer, as I often did at the time. The tiresome Celtic Tiger was rampant, and consumption was becoming a duty. But she continued, explaining that she was tidying up her will, and without putting it directly, asked if I needed anything significant when she finalised it.

I responded, 'if it's about money or property I have enough of both. If it can be bought, I'm not short of it or don't need it. But I would like a few small things from the house.' A few weeks later she came back to roughly the same conversation and she asked if I was sure about what had been said. I often reflect on how well she handled this when she was very, very unwell.

She had time and attention for everybody, would sit and chat with people, hear and understand their story and get to know them. She was unfazed when meeting the great and the good of our times, was very practical, full of common sense and waited to be asked before offering advice! It was remarkable to see her care and consideration extending to her daughters-in-law. They thanked her, at the end of her life, for being the best mother-in-law they could have wished for. She never interfered in our marriages but, if there was a bit of a tiff, she silently took the side of the wives. Perhaps her sons' wives were the daughters she never had.

She departed, as they say in the *Clare Champion*, 'ar slí na fírinne' – into the mystery of God – and in so many ways she is still with us.

And grandparents

My grandparents were all strong, distinctive people, and it would be easy to write a chapter on each of them. However here, as with my parents, the emphasis is on memories that left a strong impression – the rest, their own stories, are for another place and time. I will concentrate on my paternal grandfather and to lesser extent grandmother. However, before moving to them, a few words on the other side of the family are in order.

My maternal grandfather inherited a medium-sized land holding in north Kerry and managed it well, if slightly eccentrically. My memory is of a tall, well built, good humoured and happy man with a mischievous streak that often manifested itself when dealing with children. He had a generous nature, and when he had time, he took us out into the fields and told us grandiose stories about fairy forts and enchanted if sometimes fearful places. For much of the day he was missing, working in the fields. On Sundays, the horse and trap appeared, and he made a big fuss of getting it ready to go to mass in Brosna village which was a few miles away behind two ranges of steep hills that to a child felt like mountains.

If you were going to receive communion at Sunday mass, fasting from midnight on Saturday was mandatory, so the trip to the village was generally made without breakfast. After mass, the children were parked for breakfast with my aunt, who lived in the village. My grandfather, on the other hand, went to the pub and emerged in fine form some hours later and called at my aunt's house to pick us up. She was often disapproving of his condition. He had a tendency to go 'speeding down the village' in the horse and trap and she wouldn't allow him to take us back to the farm. Perhaps she was right as, on at least on one occasion he, the horse, the trap and the passengers all ended up over the ditch in the river at the end of the village. But that didn't change him and he remained a mischievous and happy man to the end of his days.

Granny O'Keeffe didn't come on these trips. She was different – she sat by the fire in the kitchen all the time. I never saw her move from that position and suspect an arthritic condition. She was irritable and even children took care not to cross her. Today we would suspect she was depressed, but there was little knowledge of such things then. In retrospect, it seems she gave our grandfather and many of the children a hard time.

∞   ∞   ∞

On the other side of the family, I came to know my paternal grandparents better. During the years following Grandad Malone's death, Grannie decided to convert the upper part of their house on Griffith Avenue in Dublin into a separate flat to help make ends meet during the hard times in the 1950s.

Several times a week, and daily during school holidays, I cycled from Clontarf, became the new man of the house and did much of the work involved. Now, I marvel at this but, at the time, it seemed natural. The capacity to do these things, and do them well, came from both Grandad and my father.

Grannie had an edge to her. She was efficient, business-like, anxious, impatient to get things done but always civil. She was proud of her family of origin, McGonagles from Swords. Her siblings were successful financially, in business and in the law. I suspect she also wished that for Grandad, but through a combination of nature and circumstance, it wasn't to be. Good qualities in my father and his siblings were traced by her, without exception, to the McGonagle genes. Nonetheless, she spoke of Grandad with warmth, and often related stories of how caring he was toward her.

Grandad seemed remarkably healthy, cycling everywhere when others used the bus or had cars. He had few personal needs, didn't smoke or drink and was gracious and non-judgmental in company. He would disappear on the bike, often for hours or the best part of a day. Sometimes he carried a shotgun on the bike, not something you could imagine now. When he reappeared, he would have a few rabbits or pheasants which eventually became a part of a good meal. So I was shocked when around Easter 1955, my parents, aunts and uncles scooped me up one afternoon and brought me to the Mater Hospital to attend Grandad's removal. At age seventy, he had died. Although aged ten or eleven, I've no recollection of seeing him during his final illness. Perhaps I was spared seeing his decline.

I have vivid memories of mingling, unaccompanied, in the crowd of adults outside the mortuary, walking in and out between them, only about waist high to them and not talking to anyone. I was relaxed and curious about who all the strangers were, and why they were there. Eventually, one of Grandad's sisters took charge of me. She was a quiet, unsympathetic woman with an unhealthy respect for literal truth. In the run up to a previous Christmas, she broke unwelcome news about Santa to me. She spotted I was at a loose end and took me into the mortuary. It was my first experience of seeing a dead person, a corpse – and not just any corpse but that of a deeply loved person, a cornerstone, a rock. He was recognisable, not ravaged as those who die of cancer sometimes are, but a little jaundiced. The world stopped and I ran from the mortuary. The truthful aunt would be no use. From then on, I came to regard the literal truth as something that was dangerous and needed to be dispensed with discretion; few can cope with it.

Although just entering my teens I was doing what dead grandad used do: carpentry, plumbing, painting, wallpapering, cutting and laying lino or carpet, making good the damage and so on. It seemed natural to be able to do these things – the knowledge and skill involved was absorbed effortlessly from watching Grandad and my father as they worked. Grandad was kind, gentle, unhurried and imparted knowledge and attitude with natural ease. Even more, he was slow to anger. The combination of an easy-going approach and doing things well is unusual, but it seemed natural in this tall man. It could be cutting the sole for a shoe from a sheet of leather or creating joints in pieces of wood that miraculously morphed into beautifully crafted furniture, without the intervention of nails or screws.

Rambling with him in the garden was a constant source of revelation. I recall being lifted to look closely at the blossom on trees. He observed: 'See all the little flowers, they're called apple blossom. Every one of them could become an apple. Do you think they all will?' I learned so much from the walks in the garden, seeing wood shaped, pipes being connected, water emerging from a tap in the kitchen sink that I knew came from a tank in the roof. For a boy, this was the university of life. If you were doing something the way to do it was to be relaxed, unfussed, kind and excellent.

∞   ∞   ∞

Much later, I learned that Grandad had been a member of the RIC. He and two of his brothers were serving members of the force during Easter Week 1916. He was discharged from the force with a pension in 1922. Around this time the family moved to Swords, County Dublin, where Grannie's family and siblings were prominent. I don't recall Grandad having a job, and while this may be connected to events related below, his temperament did not need an occupation to underwrite identity. Sometimes, he worked in one of the McGonagle brothers' building businesses. For example, the family house on Griffith Avenue was part of a large development undertaken by one of the McGonagles. He spent a lot of time with our family near Ennis, helping build a new house for us there, with my father.

In practice, Grannie took over the management of money. She was good at it and made sure there was enough of everything, even when it meant going out to work herself. There was something almost mystical about Grandad's benign, cultivated presence. He had a lack of connection with money worthy of a member of the British royal family. I've no recollection of seeing him handle or use it. Other relations of his generation, when visiting a house with children, would often slip a sixpenny piece or a shilling (or exceptionally a half crown) to a child. With him this didn't happen. This was not of any consequence then, but now it arouses curiosity.

∞　　∞　　∞

Half a century later the country was gripped by a craze for family history and Grandad surprised us. A search of prison registers inadvertently revealed that a James Joseph Malone was on remand in Mountjoy Jail on February 9, 1924. Checking the details confirmed this was our Grandad and started many family discussions. It appears that he was one of two arrested in the street in Swords. The other was Pat McGonagle, probably a brother of Grannie's. He was later a much-respected member of the North Dublin community. The charge was *armed hold-up and threats to shoot*. Grandad was released on bail and there is no record of any subsequent follow-up. My father was aged about seven then and could recollect seeing Grandad being arrested and led away in handcuffs, although I never heard him speak about it, but he mentioned it once to one of my siblings. At that time, Grandad was involved in a taxi business and the incident might be related to it.

Sometime after the Mountjoy revelation, I was watching a BBC 4 Scandinavian noir thriller with Lesley Malone on a Saturday evening. She lost interest and became engrossed in her laptop – I thought, correctly, it was something to do with family history. Regular exclamations of 'amazing!' and 'how interesting!' invited engagement with whatever she was finding.

I thought family history couldn't compete with the thriller. But how wrong I was. My recollection of the family history that Lesley uncovered that evening is vivid, and my memory of the Scandi thriller has vanished. She found a witness statement from the commander of the County Meath Division of the IRA, recording its activities during 1918-1921. The statements were taken by the Bureau of Military History and are available online. The commander gives descriptions of their training, manoeuvres and risks of discovery. He notes:

> There was a Constable Malone serving in the RIC and stationed in Dunshaughlin. This man was very useful to us. He had a motorcycle and usually travelled up to us in uniform with a civilian coat over his uniform. He kept us informed of all bits of information he could lay hands on, such as who was giving information to the enemy around Dunshaughlin, and the areas and persons who were wanted by the police and the houses and districts that were going to be raided. Much earlier on Malone was going to resign from the RIC but we prevailed on him not to do so, as he could render much better service to us by staying in the Force.

The likelihood is that Constable Malone was Grandad. There is no family memory relating to this, so the incident gives us a possible new side to the man I knew only in his old age. It shows how wrong it can be to feel we know somebody we have only experienced in one phase of life. On the surface at least, this and the Mountjoy incident are at variance with what I saw during his last decade. Would that we could know more, or even hear how these stories became silent. But everyone with the stories has passed on and, now, we can only look to the records. The next accidental discovery is eagerly awaited.

Homes and places

There is a sense in which the houses, flats and places we live in shape us although this is often neglected. Without doing justice to the topic here, I wish to recognise the nurturing and comforting quality many of these places had in both my personal and professional life. Some have surprising, almost anthropomorphic characteristics, and are a significant part of the story. They deserve more exploration than is practical here.

A good way to introduce the topic is to recall a conversation from a retirement dinner. On this occasion, I was seated a good distance from the centre of attention, and the speeches, none too cringeworthy, were all disposed of when we sat down, rather than at the end. By good luck, I was seated opposite a lady we will refer to as 'Mona', who was a great talker, often starting from some point in Tudor history, on which she had an endless store of knowledge, all gleaned from novels. She had a remarkable eye for eccentric detail, which made her accounts of events highly entertaining. Eventually, even the most interesting subject begins to flag, and once she registered this she moved on to talk about her house on which she was equally entertaining. It is in a small, pleasant Victorian terrace in Dublin. She loves it, quite literally, and declared:

'A man is fine for as long as he lasts – which usually isn't that long. But, the house – now that's a different kettle of fish. When you go in and close the door behind you, the house wraps itself comfortably around you, and settles you, no matter how difficult the day was. A house versus a man: it's no contest.'

And then we were regaled for the rest of the evening, leaving little doubt about the almost anthropomorphic impact of the house on her life. Men, like sundried tomatoes, were elective, okay if they were to hand, but you could get on fine without them.

When at home later, I drifted back to her theme. Some of the places I had lived in evoked similar feelings. I fell asleep thinking about this and restlessly dreamt of places lived in from my thirties. Thereafter, I began to interrogate the topic more energetically. I'd lived in more than 25 houses or apartments, and after retirement undertook an extended Camino of sorts to visit and photograph each one. They ranged from the sublime to the ridiculous, happy places and a few absorbed unhappy experiences. The nourishing quality of some of these homes was almost as important as the relationships they hosted. I read somewhere that you should *never underestimate how easily bricks and mortar can enter your soul.*

Sometimes the decision to live in a place came about very suddenly and could not have been predicted even a month earlier. Here is an example that led to two of the 25 places lived in. In 2006, after retirement, I was informally approached by one of the UN family of organisations, the International Atomic Energy Agency (IAEA) located in Vienna, with a view to taking up an appointment there (Chapters Five and Nine). The wonderful poet, Michael Longley, whose day job was as an official of the Northern Ireland Arts Council, says that retirement's gift to him was that on Monday mornings he could get up and thank the Lord that he didn't have to go to a senior staff meeting. While sharing Michael's feeling, I decided to go to Vienna to explore the situation but with little intention of accepting.

I arrived a day early and decided to visit the city's art galleries. They proved to be exceptional, and house many stunning collections from all periods of western art. The Belvedere and Leopold Galleries, among others, are home to many great works, including Gustav Klimt's now iconic *The Kiss,* and this was the first target of my visit. Less celebrated from the same period is Egon Schiele, and large collections of his work are in both galleries. Although he is sometimes known as the pornographer of Vienna, I was taken by the openness and searching quality of his work, which suggested a profound – if dark

– personal spirituality. This decided the issue, and thereafter I was lucky enough to live and work regularly in Vienna for over half a decade.

As a result, I got to know Schiele and his work exceptionally well, as a happy accident of a scientific assignment. At one stage of his life, he was so troubled by the suffering he had witnessed that he could not paint people anymore. Paradoxically, some architectural subjects he painted instead have powerful anthropomorphic qualities that are comforting in some works and menacing in others. Some have an exceptional silence and stillness, often not present in his other work. His sense of place is reminiscent of the quality Mona invested in her house. Places can acquire an aura of sanctuary, of protectiveness. They can play a special part in an individual's personal spirualty. Holy and sacred places are not always churches. Thomas Merton's writings show it is likely that even hermits' Spartan cells are comforting, and they can become quite attached to them.

The places I lived in Vienna included two beautiful city centre apartments, one in an attic situated just behind Stephansdom, the city's twelfth century gothic cathedral. From the apartment I looked down on the cathedral's ornate roof and the small, old city centre streets that were often snow-covered during the severe Austrian winter. The landlady lived in the same block and was a historian steeped in the lore of the city. For example, she explained that the large, elegant Russian restaurant across the street, which I passed every day but never saw anybody in, wasn't a restaurant at all but was simply a money laundering outfit. This fine apartment was an attractive, comfortable home, and its impact was enhanced by the rich art heritage of the city.

Somewhat different to life in Vienna, through the 1980s my family had been regular visitors to West Clare and a beautiful vacant house in a field near a house we regularly rented became available. I bought it with the agreement of the family and with some financial trepidation. It became a place of retreat and refuge from personal and professional demands. And perhaps surprisingly, it allowed my interest in set dancing and Merriman (Chapters Three and Eleven) to emerge, grow and integrate with an adult personal spirituality. Without this house, these things might not have happened.

Eventually, at the turn of the century, faced with the practical difficulties of travel and upkeep, I slowly realised that I did not need a refuge or the therapeutic comfort of the Clare house anymore. Realignment of family relationships, retirement and illnesses all played their part and it is hard to know which was cause and which was effect. The place had been vital and necessary for many years, but eventually I had outgrown it, as one grows out of living with parents. I was free to live in the city again without needing to escape from it regularly. Afterwards, I often visited the area during Merriman Summer Schools, and enjoyed fond memories of all that had happened there. I saw how the new owner was developing it, but remained grateful for the life, energy, friendships and personal growth that house had so generously hosted and nurtured. Many of the other 25 places I lived in have left a similar mark. Leaving them shares something with bereavement and is a story for another day.

Chapter Seven

Life Skills: A Sideways Look at Mitching and Meditation

Now, in old age, I am enjoying the solitude that frightened me in my youth.

– Poet Derek Mahon's reformulation of Einstein's aphorism.

Self-improvement manuals don't really cater for the unobtrusively anarchic, and thus miss some important life skills. Mitching, also known as going on the bounce, or bunking off from school, falls into this category. It evaded me as a skill until halfway through secondary school. We learn from teachers and classmates but sometimes we must discover things for ourselves, and this was the case with mitching. It did not normally come to mind, and when it occasionally raised its head it was dismissed as too risky. But, at age about fifteen, extreme practical circumstances presented themselves and no other solution was available. So, I quickly learned how to do it, with practice got good at it, and of course went on to overdo it. As T.S. Elliot explained, the only way to find out how far you can go is to go too far.

I attended Christian Brothers schools in both Ennis and Dublin and despite their reputation for being rough and abusive, this was not my experience. In O'Connell primary school, I remember only one teacher who was a little more severe in his use of corporal punishment than situations warranted. He was a young lay teacher, fresh from college, who later went on to become a national treasure and genial sports commentator with a rich, mellifluous Kerry accent: Micheál Ó Muircheartaigh. However, his excesses, if they were such, did not leave a trail of troubled memories.

During my secondary school years, we had four different Christian Brothers in charge of our class and numerous lay subject teachers. These were, with only one exception, exemplary. With the benefit of hindsight, I feel confident asserting that two of the four were saintly men of exceptional kindness, commitment and – dare I say it? – charity. The first was Brother Tracey, a tall, kind elderly man. He wore the then-normal soutane and clerical collar, and added a distinguishing eccentricity: an old, well-worn, black topcoat draped loosely over his shoulders. He smelled of pungent, raw, unsmoked and chewed tobacco. He taught English to first-year students, and memories echo of his deep resonant voice acting out parts of Robert Louis Stevenson's *Treasure Island*, our text for the year:

'I'll be as silent as the grave,' he would intone. 'Now boys, who said that?'

He took the part of Long John Silver, with a virtual crutch and a parrot on his shoulder that now seem as real as if they had existed.

Later, in fifth and sixth years, Brother Mícheál Ó Flaitile oversaw our class. A middle-aged, stocky, scholarly man, he was devoted to the Irish language through which all classes and related business were conducted. Like Brother Tracey he augmented his soutane with an additional garment, not quite a poncho, but not unlike one. Hence, he was affectionately known as Pancho, after a Mexican cartoon character in the morning newspapers. He also wore a clerical biretta, but we never figured out its significance. He took it off on entering the classroom, but shortly thereafter it was back on again and, when agitated, he fussily removed and replaced it. He was kind, a devoted teacher with huge commitments to extracurricular activities, including summer schools in the Gaeltacht, which many still remember fondly. He had infinite patience with the turbulent youths entrusted to his care, and he led a saintly life. In Irish he could be described as a '*fear uasal*', which translates as 'a man of noble character', as distinct from 'a nobleman'. A former classmate recalls that a stare from him made you question yourself but was not humiliating.

∞   ∞   ∞

The exception to this abundance of goodness, Brother Curtin, oversaw our class in third year. He was big in both height and girth and known as The Bull. He was quite unsuited to his role, but I learned a lot from him about how to deal with bullies. He had an ease with corporal punishment that none of his colleagues came close to, and went well beyond the official norm, which was limited to slapping on the hands with a short thick leather strap, referred to as *the leather*. It was a manufactured device, a little longer than a twelve-inch ruler, about the width of a bookmark and the thickness of a hamburger. In physics, quantities and measurement are always important. One slap on the open palm was known as a *biff*. Six biffs, three on each hand would be a lot in any class. But The Bull always had a leather close by and could whip it out and be in full flight at the drop of a hat. Six biffs on each hand was common, even on a good day. The real problem was that when excited by this physical exertion, or when he lost his temper, which was often, he would continue with a kind of abandon that, were it not so serious, would be comical. In this phase, he resorted to hands and fists, punching and slapping the individual involved until he calmed down.

In fairness to the school, most teachers, clerical and lay, seldom resorted to corporal punishment. During our year with The Bull, the school was being redeveloped and our class shared an exceptionally large room, back-to-back, with another class and another teacher. I have a strong memory of the horror on some other teachers' faces during The Bull's outbursts, particularly a lay Latin teacher. He sometimes stopped teaching his class and looked on in disapproving silence. But nobody had the authority or courage to intervene. What a sad commentary on a now largely forgotten aspect of life at the time.

As with most bullies, he had his favourites, notably those who were good at football. They were lucky and didn't normally attract his usual treatment. But he recruited some of these as allies to help toughen up the good players, through foul play and assault, in preparation for important games. He would beat up other unfortunate individuals, almost on sight. I was not a core member of this target group, but had a place somewhere on its fringe, and could attract his attention as he stalked the room between outbursts. This could happen if I entered his field of vision on a day when I had already produced a plausible excuse for not going to football.

The strongest memory of that year is the daily existential threat. Being in the wrong part of the classroom when the tornado struck was high risk. I tried various solutions, like doing homework, occasionally going to football, or trying to shrink into invisibility. But all of these were to no avail. It didn't matter how hard you tried – it could all come to grief very quickly unless you got out of the way. So, through fear, I started to absent myself from his classes. In doing so, I discovered the underworld of truancy for the first time and learned a lot quickly. Mitching not only avoided the savage outbursts, but it was also a cure for the boredom of some classes. At the end of third year, I did well in the Intermediate Certificate and so also learned that mitching wasn't an obstacle to getting by in exams. The adult world of experiential learning was opening up.

∞   ∞   ∞

Gradually, I learned that there were lots of ways to fill the day that were more enjoyable than school, and in fifth year I started exploring these. Some required a little money. For example, you could go to the cinema in the afternoon with no risk of meeting parents, relations, teachers et al. There were about a dozen first-run cinemas in the centre of town, and many others in the suburbs. In the morning, if the weather was bad, there was a cartoon and newsreel cinema in Grafton Street that opened early, around 10.30 am. To cover the cost, I entered the world of commerce as a helper to the local vegetable and paper delivery men, Alfie and Willie.

Then there were the cafés like Cafolla's and The Rainbow in O'Connell Street where one could nurse a cup of coffee for a few hours and listen to the top twenty played repeatedly on the ubiquitous flamboyant jukeboxes of the time. As I became more ambitious, I learned about museums and art galleries, some of which I liked. For example, I liked the Hugh Lane Gallery but found the National Gallery, at that time, to be stuffy and boring. I liked parts of the National Museum in Kildare Street but had no interest in the Dead Zoo near the Attorney General's Office. And I discovered spaces like Stephen's Green and Trinity College and came to know the centre of town well. There was an unfrequented waiting room in Connolly Station that became a meeting spot for hard core mitchers and classmates who used the train to travel into school. In good summer weather, I got as far as Dollymount Strand.

With increasing confidence, I became a more nuanced, selective and skilled mitcher during fifth and sixth years. Often, there was no need to take the full day off. I would plan to be selectively missing and discreetly slip out of the tedious classes, or to avoid embarrassment, for example, when homework wasn't done. I also graduated to more sophisticated cafes, Bewley's and Arnott's, though there was a risk of getting caught in both. My father frequented the former and my mother the latter, and I had a few near misses.

And, of course, I was eventually caught. The extent of the crime, and the level of deliberation involved, meant it couldn't be written off as a minor misdemeanour. The school principal, with whom the whole business ended up, decreed the appropriate punishment was expulsion. This was a frightening, unwelcome and unexpected reality check. As it was a first offence, or at least the first time I was caught, I was eventually dealt with leniently and allowed stay on. This was too easy and, perhaps, there should have been a seriously unpleasant punishment short of being thrown out. So, unscathed, in no time at all I was back selectively mitching, or in the popular phrase of the time, *on the bounce* again.

This time, I got away with it for the rest of fifth year, and into sixth year, and was then caught again. I was shattered and after the initial confrontation believed the game was up.

Expulsion it would be this time, and the Leaving Certificate and whatever went with it would be gone. But my parents prevailed on the saintly Brother Ó Flaitile and others to intervene with the school authorities. They succeeded and I was the unworthy recipient of the kindness of strangers. People I had not met, then or since, made an undeserved judgment in my favour that involved taking a real chance and I benefited hugely. Unfortunately, by the time I fully appreciated this, it was too late to thank them.

Mitching on a grand scale is like an entry level drug, opening new life-enhancing experiences, and at the same time being socially questionable. With practice, it became intuitive, was allowed to mutate and become integrated into adult life, with little more needed than adapting mitching skills to grown-up situations. Sometimes it carried risk and required sufficient detachment from orthodoxies to allow one to take a road less travelled. Joining the Franciscans is an example, and the decision to drop mainstream physics in favour of medical physics might, at the time, also have been seen in that light. While there is a price to be paid, mitching improves creativity and enhances one's chances of surviving difficult abusive situations.

A willingness to let go of successes achieved can be like an extension of mitching. Both involve a risk of loss or getting lost, and often require exploration of new undefined goals. Getting lost in the physical sense provides a valid metaphor for the processes of professional, personal and spiritual growth. A capacity for getting lost and letting go can be cultivated. It improves with practice and can upset those in its immediate vicinity when it begins to happen. At a dinner, some time ago, I encountered parents worried about their daughter:

'She was a model student at school,' the mother said. The father continued, 'she got straight As in all her subjects in the Leaving Certificate, almost 600 points, and got Law in Trinity.'

'Is she enjoying college life?' I enquired.

'Oh!' The mother responded. 'Well, she had good grades in the first year – not as good as at school. But now they have dropped. We're so worried about her. She could fail now. She's moved in with somebody much older, almost 30, a graduate student in Art History. Art History – I ask you! And of course, they're smoking weed.'

I nodded and waited for the story to unfold further, which it did. But I thought without saying so that there were signs of personal growth here, to which the best response might be support and encouragement. Worry was unlikely to help. From the other end of the table, a quiet, slightly dishevelled man who hadn't said much piped up: 'Sounds to me like she's growing up at last.'

Of course, this wasn't well received, and the conversation veered in another direction linked to the dishevelled man's life as a priest.

∞　　∞　　∞

Once I was established as head of a small department, in the late 1970s or early 1980s, two adult versions of mitching emerged. Initially, I did not recognise these for what they were. The first was a habit of just going missing for a while, as a pressure relief valve. If the going got unreasonably tough within the department, or from external sources such as hospital management or clinicians, I would simply take off. It was a time of enormous developments in Irish hospitals, and in many supporting services including medical physics. New scientific and technical problems appeared relentlessly. My therapy for this was to depart to Bewley's, and from there consider whatever needed attention, read what needed to be read, or allow problems to solve themselves unbidden. And, of course, like the best, I also read novels and poetry there. After all, it was Bewley's, and good manners dictated that one did so, as well as reading *The Irish Times* occasionally. Even a saint would be improved by being there. The outcome was good solutions to problems that might otherwise have become chronic ones.

As responsibilities grew I would, when exasperated with colleagues, slip away from the department and indulge in the second form of adult mitching. I went to the cinema (often the Screen) or for a walk by the sea or a similar activity totally detached from work. At one point, a liking developed for the college library's early printed books room, where I was introduced to and became immersed in Robert Boyle's numerous works. He was an under-acknowledged architect of the British Enlightenment and the primacy of the observable. He was mocked by Hobbes and the German mathematician Leibniz, who believed Boyle wasted his time trying to establish by observation/experiment what they (Leibniz et al.) knew to be true by the faculty of reason alone. He was deeply religious in a stoic Anglican way, and his scientific observation and religious practices were both equally rigorous and inspired. Reading first-hand of his experimental rigour and unbounded curiosity was always a refreshing break.

To be free to do all this effectively required a special facility: an office with two doors. In both hospital and university life, I was lucky enough to be able to arrange this. It meant one could escape from a secretary whose duty included organising

Sfera con Sfera *by Arnoldo Pomodoro. Trinity College Dublin.*
Photograph courtesy of Lilly Markovic and the author.

Pat Plunkett holding forth in the Royal College of Surgeons, Dublin

*Former TCD Medical School Deans circa 1980 to 2006. Photo 2002.
(top row) John Bonnar, Ian Temperley RIP, Dermot Hourihane RIP,
Davis Coakley RIP, (bottom row) Derry Shanley, the author,
and James McCormick RIP*

Some Department Heads and Valerie Kampf, PA to the Dean, circa 2003. From left (STANDING): Professors Eoin Gaffney (Pathology), John Clarkson (Dental Affairs), John Reynolds (Surgery, James's), Derry Shanley (Dean), Colm O'Morain (Medicine, Tallaght), Dermot Kelleher (Medicine, James's), Nicky Kennedy (Human Nutrition), Kevin Conlon (Surgery, Tallaght), Bernard Walsh (Medicine for Elderly), (SITTING): Michael Cullen (Chairman, Medical Board, James's), the author (retiring Dean), and Davis Coakley RIP (former Dean).

Canto de Synnaquir, *by Antonio Máro. International Atomic Energy Agency*

St Francis and the Birds *by Helmar Hillebrand.*
International Atomic Energy Agency. (Flash photography used)

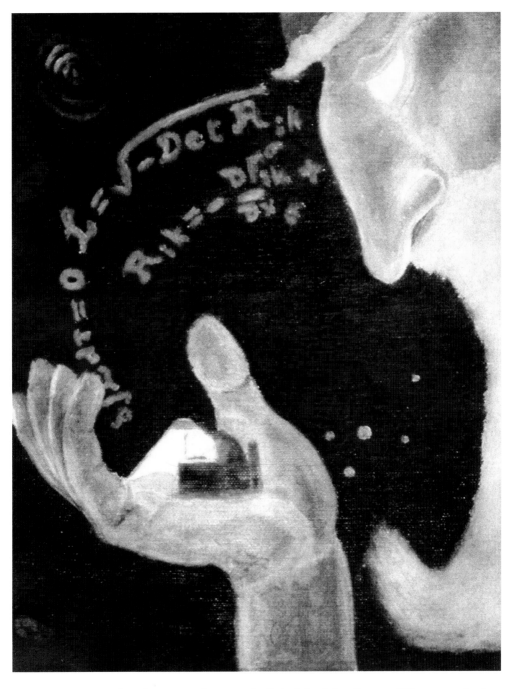

Discovery in Schrödinger in the Hand of God *by John Synge (Circa 1940/50).*
Dublin Institute for Advanced Studies (DIAS). Photograph courtesy of
Lilly Markovic and the author.

Woman Emerging *by Edwina Sands, International Atomic Energy Agency –
man included to give perspective on scale of the work*

Irene Martin and Mary Friel, doyens of Brooks Academy (of set dancing).
On top of Mount Callan, the eponymous Mist Covered Mountain
overlooking the Willy Clancy Summer School, early 1990s

Betty McCoy at Merriman, 1991

Michael Tubridy (with glasses), Betty McCoy (in sunglasses) and Ciaran Mac Mathuna at Connie Ryan's Funeral, Clonoulty, 1999

one's life and knowing how one could be contacted. There was little prospect of encountering troublesome or demanding colleagues at the Screen cinema or the other protected places I came to frequent. Much later, I became a little concerned about bumping into students when at the cinema, but don't recall ever doing so. Being able to occasionally take off in this way was greatly assisted by working in multiple locations (several hospitals and the college). I had a free heart and felt no guilt about such absences. The time lost (if one took a narrow view of the situation) was more than compensated for by the 10 to 12-hour days that became part of hospital life.

A habit of opting to meet colleagues in their offices, rather than suggesting mine, also helped. In practice, I usually started the day at my own office and dealt with any local problems. Thereafter, the rest of the day was spent out and about, at meetings, working on projects, visiting new developments, at coffee and so on. This had many advantages and one learned with precision what was working and what was not. And the periods spent in the cinema, the library, Bewley's or walking to and fro across large campuses allowed creative solutions to come to fruition.

Absence is a gift that a head should confer on a department. It allows individual members to grow and take responsibilities that an ever-present head might hoard to themselves. The net result of absences was that many individuals stepped up, responded to opportunities, and grew. Not everybody was so inclined, and some found not having the head around all the time stressful and longed for a more protected environment. So, I tried to create an atmosphere where both the overtly ambitious and the more guarded felt they would be protected even if they made serious errors but were acting in good faith. To support this, we evolved an unconventional, flat management structure that served us well and lasted until the department grew to about forty members, at which time I left.

On a different note, adult mitching eventually provided the opportunity to realise that my primary interest was no longer in managing the day-to-day work of the department or those working in it. My real interest was working collaboratively with talented people on the constant stream of innovation and new activities that it was our privilege to be part of. Both medical physics and engineering offered endless opportunities for development, and the health service in Ireland was undergoing its own renaissance. All that was required was an open-ended, energetic, imaginative commitment and good colleagues.

Years later, on returning to work after several weeks of serious illness – a heart attack – I vividly recall walking through the main foyer in St James's Hospital. The most striking memory is of sensory overload. I was in my fifties and accustomed to lots of interaction with people. Many in the foyer greeted me with a 'hello' and 'welcome back'. Some mentioned problems and others shared solutions to old dilemmas. It continued through the day, endless, pleasant, undemanding interaction – low-key – but I was overwhelmed. By lunchtime, I was exhausted, ironically, by a positive social experience.

The weeks of convalescence had unexpectedly been a welcome experience. I was surprised not to miss the cut and thrust of day-long, full-on interaction with people. Recuperation had been solitary and rewarding, allowing a natural ease with solitude to be indulged. It had almost always been possible to take walks alone without being regarded as eccentric. But an unexpected source of solitary time was conferences. Medical physics was a relatively new field and, for decades, I was the only Irish delegate at its international conferences. Dinners and receptions were hit and miss affairs, particularly in the early days. One could end up seated in a spare place on a table with no English speakers. Mitching from these occasions provided opportunities for quiet time when one was so inclined.

But even with regular absences from the dinner table, effective international networks developed and conferences became more demanding. I decided to reduce their impact by not attending any receptions as well as passing on most formal dinners. Either could consume much of an evening. But if one was deeply involved in the organisation of an event, there was little choice and attendance was mandatory. However, not being a complete hermit, when opportunity allowed, I opted for the real alternative of informal meals with a few colleagues. These were seldom less than enjoyable, seeded many friendships and were often professionally rewarding. Brendan Kennelly, commenting on a presidential reception he had attended in Dublin Castle, declared that it 'wasn't a patch on a fair day in Listowel or Ballylongford'. I tend to agree.

I continue to feel no obligation to attend receptions and seldom do so. Being host to continuous back pain since 1990 does not help, and few things exacerbate it more than standing around for over an hour. In addition, for almost three decades, I was a paid-up member of the unruly prostate and diuretic swigging communities. While receptions and dinners are not off limits to those enjoying these conditions, they do little to calm their demands and nothing to make them enjoyable.

Nevertheless, as a species, we have an inherent desire to see or meet iconic figures. The late Pope John Paul and President Kennedy are examples. I saw both in the flesh, over a decade apart, at almost the same spot in Dublin city centre.

President Kennedy passed by in his motorcade roughly where the Trinity Luas stop is now, and the late pope whizzed by the corner of D'Olier Street and the quays. I'm glad I saw both in the flesh. Many other sightings occurred over the years, including President Obama almost a lifetime later. But I never aspired to meet and converse with such figures even if the opportunity presented itself, as it did with Nelson Mandela and Mikhail Gorbachev. Both were compelling figures. It was special to be in the same room as them and see them moving around greeting people. While in awe of their achievements, I knew meeting them would be a glancing, rather fake encounter. The more distant experience of sharing in their presence at a formal meal seemed preferable.

However, inadvertent handshakes with the great and the good are an unavoidable hazard of attendance at functions, and I accepted these with good grace. A memorable one was with Ban Ki Moon, former Secretary General of the United Nations. He regularly visited the UN building in Vienna and held 'town hall'-style staff meetings there. One such meeting was scheduled in a large central lobby space around the time I normally passed through it on the way to lunch. I decided to go to lunch late to avoid this meeting. On my way, I entered the lobby close to the podium, just as a well-dressed Asian gentleman stepped from the platform and approached me to shake hands. I assumed the person was part of a project in the building and was just being sociable. But Ban Ki Moon it was, and he moved quickly on to the next willing hand, after a simple greeting. We are only six handshakes away from anybody on the planet. So, what's the big deal? Better to shake our colleague's or neighbour's hand and embrace them.

∞　　∞　　∞

For many, solitary time can lead to meditation, mindfulness and retreats, and over the years I have spent time on all three. Meditation is a weasel word: it can mean many different things. But there is a constant that involves regularly moving away from the hurly-burly of daily life for at least 20 to 30 minutes a day. And that is enough to keep many people from it.

In the Franciscans we were introduced to a formulaic approach to meditation. It was scheduled for the whole community every morning and evening, during which we sat in neat silent rows in the chapel. It was highly cognitive: after settling down, you took a topic (for example, forgiveness) or an incident from the gospels or other reading, and examined it mentally for a while, reflected on it, and explored how it might be applied to a situation you were familiar with. It ended with a few resolutions on what you might do about it in practice, and a prayer.

It was like a cross between cognitive psychotherapy and a business school project management exercise, with the added possibility of divine intervention. Most of the meditation period was spent on the impossible task of trying to discipline the mind from wandering. At that time, eastern approaches and mindfulness had not yet found their place in the west. Our young Franciscan minds were filled with distractions and fantasies and the tools offered to deal with them were willpower and prayer; neither was much good.

One of the Franciscan students was regularly agitated at evening meditation. Whatever he was struggling with manifested itself in a kind of displacement and physical rocking to and fro, accompanied by noisy exhalations. His agitation disturbed the normally deep silence of the session: very distracting for those on either side or behind him. Eventually, the senior priest sitting behind him broke the silence and hissed:

'Oh, for God's sake! Give in to it, whatever it is.'

A titter ran around the assembly, and that did for the rest of that session.

Deeper and more 'advanced' adventures in meditation were mentioned from time to time in classes. But these were regarded as the preserve of mystics, and we were told that if we worked hard for half a lifetime we might (but probably wouldn't) reach such exotic heights. In retrospect this wasn't a good approach. It reflected the interest of the church(es) in controlling what one's mind was allowed to experience, and direct (mystical) experience of God was not to be trusted. While the Catholic Church allowed for it, it liked to have the experience expressed in theological language which rendered it safe, inaccessible and uninteresting. This created an additional problem for women mystics, as the church had not allowed women to study theology over the centuries. Thus, with less than a handful of exceptions, the experience of women mystics was sidelined – a great loss to the wider community, particularly as mystical experiences may be more common among women.

Alternative approaches to meditation, common in eastern traditions, have been enthusiastically taken up in the west. Their rise in Ireland almost mirrors the decline in the 'faith of our fathers'. They start from techniques that calm the mind using, for example, observation of the breath or a mantra. Mindfulness is an abstracted version of this. It is a 'low fibre' form of mind calming without any (disturbing religious) content. Many find it helps navigate life. Twenty minutes of mindfulness and most people can, with practice, approach a still mind and may begin to be open to things that need to be attended to but often don't reach consciousness. Much good can flow from this. But a mind that has never been still can be seriously challenged by this experience, and the first steps are best taken with a good mentor or teacher. Notwithstanding this, a quiet mind opens the door to real adventure in both the sciences and in the spiritual life (Chapters Five and Nine). It is the place where scientific genius may receive the insight that alters how we see things. It is also the place where the mystics have profound experiences or contact with whatever lies beyond. Though real, their experience is more difficult to share.

Retreats are a natural extension of the reflective/cognitive forms of meditation as well as the openness to receptive processes that can be a prelude to the mystical. Many structures have evolved around retreats, ranging from solitary to community forms, with or without talks, with individual or collective guidance, and spread over periods from a day or two up to several weeks. Whatever the form, they usually involve some 'retreating' from the preoccupations of daily life, that is, mitching. One of the more demanding is the 30 days of silence in the well-regarded Jesuit spiritual exercises.

In midlife, I visited Glenstal and Melifont Abbeys several times annually. These unguided retreats usually lasted two to four days. They involved long solitary walks that slowed one down and gave space to reflect and integrate whatever was going on in life. The abbeys also had the daily round of liturgy, executed with reverence, particularly in Glenstal. About half a dozen times a day the monks assembled to chant the divine office. Well-practised male voices in a large church are special, moving and echo long after one has left the monastery. No doubt something similar can be said about visits to female monastic communities, for example, the Poor Clares. I occasionally brought family or friends to visit Glenstal, usually for the late morning daily high mass with all the bells and smells. Visitors always came away moved and impressed.

Gradually, from about my mid-fifties onward, I started to substitute solitary time for monastic retreats. This was spent in the house in Clare or during extended periods of lone travelling (Chapter Eight). Both are compatible with the mood of retreat, and the periods involved are generally longer than the times spent in monasteries. Though I enjoy having more time, I miss the framework of liturgy, chant and communal silence.

Retirement involves letting go on a grand scale and seems like mitching for ever more. At a retirement function, I was surprised to hear my successor comment that it required courage to take the job I had been doing, given that I had just had a heart attack. On the contrary, thoughts in that vein had not crossed my mind. I had sized up the situation, felt the job was worth doing and that I could do it – heart attack and all. But I resolved that for as long as the job was enjoyable, I would do it, but if the *joie de vivre* of the challenge departed, then so would I, and this eventually happened. When the time came to let go, I recall that it took more courage to retire than it had taken to start.

Something happened shortly after the heart attack that strangely paved the way for letting go. On return to work, I found much more than the sensory overload already mentioned. This included a level of protection by my PA/secretary, Juliet Bite, and by other staff. At the time, I only half noticed the support they so generously gave. But on being told about it later, I was both alarmed and humbled. Her response to phone enquiries went something like this:

'Hello. Medical Physics. How can we help you?'

'This is Dr Grey speaking. Can I speak to Professor Malone please?'

'He's not available just now. Can I help?' She responds.

'Thanks for the offer, but I need to speak with him directly!'

'Could you try ringing back later this morning?'

'Will he be around this afternoon?'

'No. Of course not. He takes a nap after lunch.'

'Well, tomorrow morning then?'

'Yes, try then. And listen! You're not to be annoying him. He's not well you know and you're not to annoy him. Are you sure I can't help?'

The care and solicitude of several members of the department was special. It is now more memorable than the dutiful good wishes that I was also happy to receive. I treasure how special it felt as I unsteadily moved into a demanding new role, at a time when I might just as easily have been dead. However, accepting and relaxing into this care was not without complication. It implied another dimension of 'letting go', that is, of the deference attached to professional/academic roles.

The grand flowering of 'letting go' was on October 4, 2002, retirement at age 58, with indifferent health, into a largely unknown, unpredictable future, which turned out to be wonderful. It was the natural culmination of a life of learning to let go of successes and bothersome failures in favour of the unknown, and started from the mitching gene. Some observers rated this move as a bad one. But it has been more rewarding than anything that could have been anticipated, or that might have been foreseen, had I stayed safely put.

EXTRA CURRICULAR

Chapter Eight

Over the Hills: Kuwait – Luxembourg on the Gulf – and Yemen

Life is generally something that happens elsewhere.

– Alan Bennett

Some feel the collective noun for professors should be an absence. They are often delighted to be invited to travel. Many trips are just routine, just involving conferences and meetings. However, others, even if exotic, can be risky and uncomfortable as will be seen in this account of visits to two countries, Kuwait and Yemen.

Kuwait is a small country at the apex of the Persian Gulf and had a population of about 2.1 million in 1990, sixty per cent of whom were foreign nationals. At the time, it reputedly held about 20 per cent of the world oil reserves, which gave its tiny native population unparalleled wealth. Inevitably, it attracted large numbers of expat professionals, particularly Palestinians, to help implement the development that wealth on this scale made possible. In addition, large numbers of domestics and servants were attracted from the Far East. Looking at it on the map, one sees a small Luxembourg-shaped triangular wedge of territory sitting between Iraq and the sea.

Yemen, when I visited it about ten years later, had over ten times Kuwait's population: about 25 million and almost all native. It is situated at the far end of the Gulf. Although it borders Saudi Arabia, it has little oil wealth. However, it was and is an exotic place. Its capital Sana'a has special architecture not to be seen anywhere else. Its politics were unique, leaving it barely governable and with an energetically closed society. It was alone in offering sanctuary to the Iraqi dictator, Saddam Hussein. All women including professionals wore full burqa outside the home.

I started to visit Kuwait in the mid-1980s, generally in two-week blocks. Once there, the onerous duties involved giving one, or at most two, lectures a day. Initially this was boring, and two weeks felt like a long sentence as there was little to see or do there. For much of the year, even going out for a walk was not practical, given the extreme temperatures. But life there was peaceful, and once one adapted to the surroundings, they afforded an opportunity for something close to a retreat. Mind you, it was a retreat in the comfortable surroundings of five-star accommodation, with a driver to shepherd one, without having to navigate the strangeness of Kuwait City, the surrounding desert, and the crazy local traffic problems. So, with experience, I adapted and generally looked forward to the visits, which became a mixture of quiet time/retreat, punctuated by intense local engagement. This attractive idyll was disrupted by the 1990 Iraqi invasion and the subsequent wars and instability in the Gulf area. But it was particularly interesting to see this small country in its natural state before destabilisation by these events.

Prior to 1990, there was an ongoing, gradual liberalisation of life and social mores in Kuwait. Though this was most evident among younger women, all of society was touched by it. At that time, there was a pervasive sense among many visitors that the place was unreal, interactions were unreal, and projects were managed with an ingrained unreality. The liberalisation had in part to do with an emerging openness, but also related to a wider commitment to building a place that could be genuinely good to live in. Unfortunately, Saddam Hussein's invasion and the first war set these movements back years, if not decades. Exploration of new freedoms was abandoned, and the safer default of the old ways prevailed.

Before the war, most women wore long dresses and a headscarf that hid their hair. A small proportion wore western dress and did not seem to be challenged when they did so. Unlike in Saudi Arabia or Yemen, few wore the full, long black burqa or covered their faces. After the war, all Kuwaiti women dressed modestly, and only foreigners dressed in the western style, and often even foreign women wore headscarves, especially if going to the souk or for a walk. There was a reappearance of the full burqa, but it did not become the dominant dress style as it was in Yemen (below).

Men went through similar though less noticeable changes. Before the war, the proportion wearing Arab dress progressively declined so that by the end of the eighties a majority wore smart, casual western dress in the medical school. After the war, the proportion wearing Arab dress increased. The least likely to wear Arab dress, among those indigenous to the region, were Palestinians, Egyptians and Bahrainis.

The weather in Kuwait was then probably among the most inclement on earth. Temperatures soar in the summer months, well into the 40s, and can approach 50°C. And this is augmented by a phenomenon like sandstorms, but with the refinement that the particles are so small that they can penetrate indoors even through air conditioning filtration systems. For those sensitive to it, this results in sore, irritated throats as with a bad cold. The net outcome is that many depart to more clement climates during the summer months (June to August).

But putting climate aside, Kuwait was not then and still is not a normal place. Many examples could be cited, but three will suffice. The first is segregation of audiences at the cinema. For some showings, you could go as a family but could not attend as a single man. Single men had special 'bachelor' showings that were designed to keep the sexes apart.

Another example occurred when the head of a university department requested me to host a PhD candidate in Dublin. I requested a meeting with the candidate, which was part of our normal process. The meeting was arranged, and a young woman, the candidate, arrived accompanied by her brother, a young doctor, whose job was to vet me on behalf of the family. She was very bright, and we agreed to accept her. She arrived to our department in St James's Hospital accompanied by both her brother and her father. They both sat outside every day and accompanied her to and from work. Within a month she gave in to the pressure and was whisked back to Kuwait, married, and never seen again.

Finally, after visiting a very well-equipped department, I asked why there were two CT scanners. It seemed the workload would not even keep one busy. The reply was that at the time of purchase a clerical error had resulted in two being ordered. An attempt was made to correct the situation but it was unsuccessful as the administration discreetly advised that 'the bribe had already been received' in respect of both machines, and couldn't be returned.

There are few, if any, tourists in Kuwait, and a visa is required to enter (and leave), with the result that both are valued and carefully looked after. For example, during the first war, those who did not need to be there or were regarded as politically unreliable still needed an exit visa to leave. I had the strange experience of being on holiday in Clare when the invasion happened in early August 1990. That year I was scheduled for a short visit in September. The invasion was so disruptive that all activity of that type was cancelled, and there was huge pressure on expats to leave the country. A serious problem was that many did not have visas and most of the administrative arrangements for issuing them were defunct. Thus, exit visas became highly treasured items. When I returned to Dublin at the end of August after the holidays, I found a letter from the Kuwaiti Embassy in London in the pile of neglected post. It contained both an entry and exit visa for the now cancelled trip. They had been issued a couple of days prior to the invasion. There was something fascinating about them and I had them framed. They still hang on the wall in my kitchen as a reminder of how fast even apparently stable things change, and how something we barely think about becomes vitally important.

It took some time to develop a few social connections there, even when visiting regularly. But once things settled down, I was invited to dinner more frequently than in any other place, apart from Galway in the late 1970s and 1980s. In Galway, it was down to one relentlessly hospitable radiologist, Harry McMahon, who ensured one was generously and graciously entertained. In Kuwait, I was eventually entertained in many people's homes, but the great majority were expats.

The style of entertainment varied enormously. In some houses, the whole family would join in an evening meal, whereas in others the women were excluded and only the men and perhaps some colleagues sat with the guests. From among the Middle Eastern peoples, I found the Palestinians and the Egyptians to be the best hosts, although I have fond memories of evenings spent in Iraqi, Syrian, British and Australian homes. Some houses observed the 'dry' laws of the state, but many would discretely let it be known that booze was available if desired. Others seemed to be able to maintain almost a full bar, which was quite an achievement. I recall a celebrated hospital consultant leaving the plane in Kuwait City's 35° plus heat wearing a long winter overcoat equipped with numerous *naggin*-sized pockets. As he clanked toward safety beyond the customs officers his illicit cargo could amply stock any home bar. On the other hand, an Irish Labour Party Health Minister was intercepted red handed there, for a minor infringement, and given a lecture on the moral evils of drink.

Markers for extraordinary wealth were present everywhere in Kuwait. As the impact of the war declined and the 1990s advanced, some of these became more and more obvious. For example, trees that lined the middle of a road I travelled every day to the medical school had to be kept alive with a formal sophisticated process of artificial irrigation. The driver, a Syrian, with a jaundiced take on much that happened in Kuwait, always declared on passing these trees, 'They're not trees – they're dinars [the national currency].'

∞   ∞   ∞

An exception to this open, big-hearted hospitality among expats was an invitation to dine with a high-born Kuwaiti, whom we will refer to as 'Dr Khaled Al Sayer', at his desert villa. The invitation came during the initial phase of a new programme and involved several senior figures from the Dublin medical schools. Some importance was attached to the occasion and our party of about eight assembled punctually in the lobby of the hotel where we were staying and waited for Dr Al Sayer to collect us. The arranged time came and went, and there was no sign of our host. It was early evening, and we heard the call to prayer, which also came and went and still no sign. Some of our party became restive; after all, they were no shrinking violets, and some had egos that did not like to be kept waiting.

It is perhaps necessary to mention that Dr Al Sayer had been a trainee specialist in one of the Dublin hospitals. He had been unhappy there, failed the exams and had recently returned to Kuwait, where his status improved significantly due to his family's position. But the party was not pleased to be kept waiting by a junior doctor who had failed his exams, even if he was a big shot in Kuwait. About 10 minutes after the call to prayer Dr Al Sayer, with two or three acolyte chauffeurs, all in Arab dress, breezed into the lobby. He made a theatrical apology for having been delayed by the prayers, emphasising the sense of duty involved. He distributed the guests between the chauffeurs, and the party departed. I had not been allocated to any of the departing cars and he looked me in the eye and said: 'Now, Dr Malone, you and I can travel together.'

I began to feel uneasy. If anyone were to travel with him, it should have been somebody more senior from our party. Also, I was an examiner at an oral session he did not do well in and had been a member of the board that failed him. Surprisingly, the exchanges as we walked to the car were relaxed. But the subsequent journey was one of the most memorable and frightening I'd experienced in over a decade of visits to troubled parts of the world. Darkness had fallen, and I found myself on a terrifying trip through the desert followed by an alarming high-speed journey along motorways once we left the city. At one stage we appeared to go up an exit ramp and appeared to join a motorway going in the wrong direction. In retrospect, the only explanation I can think of is that it might have been a new road not yet open to traffic that he knew was safe. At other stages, he left the road and drove out into the desert. If we survived, I wondered if the destination might be a basement in Beirut.

Eventually, we left the motorway and after travelling through what seemed like open desert in the dark, arrived at an oasis of light: Dr Al Sayer's villa. The lighting arrangements would have provided stiff competition with some of the more garish domestic Christmas displays seen in housing estates in Dublin suburbs. But I was glad to see it and re-join the rest of our party, whose journeys had been less eventful. What followed was an ostentatious display of power and wealth.

After we were greeted, it became clear Dr Al Sayer's wife would not be joining us, even though I seem to remember she made an appearance and had a role in supervising the banquet. We were all seated at a long, elaborately decorated table set with what seemed to be gold cutlery and weighed down with food of every sort in the Middle Eastern style. Dr Al Sayer presided at one end. The atmosphere was at best uneasy, and he explained that we should eat our fill as being abstemious would be offensive (there was no alcohol). The last thing I felt like was eating, and some others clearly felt the same, but over the next two hours we had to eat up like bold children as more and more exotic dishes were piled onto the groaning table.

Eventually he declared dinner was over, and we moved into a reception room furnished with long, low divan sofas. After we were seated, two servants arrived with censors and incensed each person thoroughly, to the extent that the smell impregnated our clothing. The atmosphere remained tense as Dr Al Sayer began circulating. He eventually arrived at the sofa I was seated on and perched on the arm at the end.

'Dr Malone, the summer exam was very difficult,' he said. The room became quiet, and attention focused on him.

'It was the London Royal College's exam, not mine,' I replied.

'Still, it was exceedingly difficult, and some might feel the results including the viva were racist.'

'Of course it was a difficult exam,' I replied, 'and a lot of people have to try more than once to pass. As for racism, I am sure if you look at the list of candidates who have passed over the years, you will find people from every background.'

'Even so, it was a very difficult exam, Dr Malone,' he responded with a satisfied little smile. And he moved on.

The atmosphere in the room relaxed. Dr Al Sayer was an intense, committed, religious, scrupulous man of modest talents, who had succeeded in qualifying as a doctor. He and his family were determined he would succeed, but things were more difficult than anticipated. He had asserted his position as far as a troublesome conscience would allow. He had metaphorically thrown the rattle out of the cot and that was it.

There was, however, a sequel. Some days later, he showed up and invited a colleague and I to accompany him to a camel auction. Camel auctions were popular at the time in Kuwait, like the fair day in a town. I was initially nervous, but it became obvious that he was repairing fences. So we headed off, had a great day and experienced the sights, smells and buzz of the auction, which was something to remember.

There was an insidious, barely visible form of deprivation in Kuwait, and a talented group that suffered its more extreme form. They were the professional middle class, highly skilled, well qualified and often Palestinian. They were key to keeping universities, hospitals, schools, businesses, and public administration going. These, the urbane high achievers, dominated professional life, but they were not allowed to buy property or become citizens in Kuwait. They devoted long service to the country, sometimes lifelong, and were its stable backbone. And so, it is unsurprising that many of them did not have a sense of belonging. Inevitably, when the Iraqi invasion came, their loyalty could not be taken for granted. This had a huge impact and eventually led to mass expulsion/exodus overland through 'safe corridors' to the Mediterranean. At the time, the exit visa hanging on my wall as a conversation piece might have proved invaluable to any one of them.

There was another dimension to the poor treatment of the Palestinians and other professional expats. In the work environment, though charged with a lot of responsibility, they were often rendered dependent on less talented native Kuwaiti citizens, who were the official bosses in most enterprises. In addition, at least two salary scales were in operation for every job in professional areas, one for Kuwaiti citizens and another for the rest. The Kuwaiti salary was generally twice that for expats, and the differential could be even more. Expat salaries were further differentiated, with Europeans and those from the US tending to be paid more than those from Africa,

Asia, Eastern bloc countries or the Russian Federation. This was only slightly more extreme than the disempowerment experienced by illegals in the US. The reasons for the long-term failure to resolve the US problem may well have roots that are not dissimilar to those that sustained the abusive system in Kuwait.

Large numbers of domestic servants were also 'imported' from the Far East, particularly Sri Lanka, the Philippines, India and to a lesser extent the neighbouring states of Iraq and Syria. Most families, including Europeans, had servants at that time. At dinner one evening, an Iraqi host explained that even before the war, this was a source of great resentment rooted in history. For generations the order of things was that poor Kuwaitis migrated to Baghdad in Iraq to work as servants, labourers and domestics. The notion of a poor Kuwaiti had become an oxymoron and then the flow reversed, so that now Iraqis often moved to Kuwait City for professional and domestic jobs. Shades of the migration patterns between Ireland and London. There was a strong sense among Iraqis and Syrians that the real destiny of Kuwaitis was to be servants and underlings in Baghdad and Damascus. A casual look at the map will reinforce the view held by many Iraquis, that is, that Kuwait is a province of Iraq. They also firmly believed that Kuwaitis were an inferior people.

With wealth, huge shopping malls sprang up with the most exotic designer brands. Expensive cars and luxurious indulgences were on public display everywhere. These existed side by side with relative deprivation, some of it not visible. Asian domestics supported the system of privilege. But, looking back, the extent of inequality and deprivation was less visible than that seen in major American cities like Chicago or New York. There was a sense in which the Kuwaiti state looked after those who were useful to its objectives. But once this condition was not fulfilled, they were surplus to requirements and shipped back home.

The souk or city market was a marvellous place, and once I got comfortable going out alone, I often went there. You could buy anything and ended up having strange conversations with locals who did not have good information from outside the country. It was still before widespread internet access. Among the most extraordinary things I recall were the money shops. Most people received their wages in cash, in Kuwaiti dinars (KD), then an in-demand hard currency and worth about €2.50. Foreigners were shy about displaying the wedge of cash they received each week or month, whereas others enjoyed looking at it and counting it. There was a special liturgy among locals around counting large bundles of notes, which I haven't seen elsewhere. The notes slid over each other and magically separated. They danced and flickered and crackled through practiced, experienced, skilful fingers with unnerving speed, almost as fast as the machines now often seen in the background to financial reports on TV.

Many people, particularly Asians, had arrangements to send money to their families every month, and the business of currency exchange in the souk's money shops was something special. Changing currency at a bank or hotel was for softie westerners: the money shops were frequented by most others and were unique. You could change KD for any currency you can imagine, and some you never heard of. All the well-known currencies were there, including dollars, sterling, deutschmarks and later the euro. But there were also dozens of currencies from smaller countries.

The money shops had their own area, a couple of streets, each no longer than a Luas tram. Each shop was about the size of a small sweetshop. A short counter displayed the currencies and one or two men sat behind it. In the middle distance the displays looked like stacks of chocolate bars in a glass cabinet, but as you approached the stacks morphed into colourful bundles of bank notes. No security, no alarm bells, no armed guards, no reinforced glass windows and microphone between you and the man behind the counter. The 'shopkeepers' were a curious cross between village grocer and bookie's clerk, assessing the odds with each customer. For them, no deal was too small, and as I found out, it would be hard to propose a deal that would be too big. They were dressed, as were most locals, in Arab dress – the full white tunic (*dishdasha*) and headscarf (*keffiyeh*).

I was browsing in the money shop area one evening when two Arab men entered one of the little shops toting a medium-sized plastic grocery bag. It was full of bundles of KD notes. They indicated the amount involved and that they wanted to exchange it for US dollars. The shopkeeper offered each a little glass of sweetened mint tea and, after what appeared like family greetings, got to negotiating a rate, which was struck as quickly as in a fruit or vegetables purchase. The US dollars, about a quarter of a million of them, were tabled and replaced the dinars in the plastic bag. All were satisfied, the deal was done, and everybody seemed to go about the rest of their day without feeling anything remarkable had happened – that is, except me. I still find it extraordinary that such a large deal could be done without security, and identity checks, and proof of address and so on. In Dublin, I recently requested a significant withdrawal from a city centre branch of my own bank. The teller responded, without even a glimmer of recognition of the irony involved: 'But you can't do that here. This is a cash-free bank.'

The Kuwaiti money shop men could teach our bankers a thing or two.

∞ ∞ ∞

Thinking about Kuwait brings back so many memories, moods and contradictions. At one level, the people are resourceful and ingenious in unexpected ways, as was illustrated in their capacity to deal with the burning oil wells in the desert. They were torched by the retreating army and the Americans had offered the legendary Red Adair to deal with them at outrageous expense. But the locals were not to be outwitted by their liberators and slipped off to find a group of Eastern Europeans who did it at a fraction of the price in a fraction of the time.

At another level, I always had a feeling the place was artificial and did not really exist. There were so many constraints on interaction between people and the way life functioned. And yet the gloves came off now and then and 'inhibited' is not an adjective that can describe Arabs in full flow exchanging insults. There is a very full and rich culture there, and its main weakness is that it is 'exclusive' in the literal sense. It excludes the other, the foreigner, the infidel. There is a powerful sense of family, which has many good features but can also be deeply controlling and toxic, as it was to the young woman who tried and failed to break away to do a PhD.

Much later, when all this was only a memory, I had occasion to revisit Kuwait for the United Nations. Regardless of all the implied criticism above, one thing became clear during this visit: the hospitality of the Kuwaiti ministry had been far better than that of the UN. International civil servants do not always have a privileged lifestyle during such visits. The city felt much as it had twenty years earlier, but the good and the bad features were sharper. The wealth was just as obvious, even more so in the architecture of many new malls. Likewise, the exclusion of some groups was clearer.

On return to Dublin from this visit, I was contacted on behalf of a colourful Mayo businessman. He had thoughts of converting some large hotel buildings in Kuwait City into a hospital. On his behalf, I was persuaded to host the Kuwaiti Minister for Health to a lunch. This created an interesting challenge in managing opulence and exclusion, Irish-style. The minister proved to be a difficult guest to engage until we moved the conversation to his specialty, bariatric surgery. I don't quite know why, but there is something particularly apt about that as an end to the Kuwaiti story.

∞　　∞　　∞

Although in the same geographic region as Kuwait, Yemen, in the first decade of the new century, was unique and quite different. For example, it was alone in offering sanctuary to Saddam Hussein, and was willing to receive his body after execution. It was a country of circa 25 million people, outside the norm in its politics, barely governable, and a definitively closed society. This applied not only to visitors from the west, but also to Arab neighbours. It was also under the influence of Moscow and seemed to remain there after the USSR's collapse. It is now paying a dreadful price for its separation from the rest of the world. But prior to this catastrophe, it was a strange and exotic place to visit.

I was dispatched there around 2007/08 by the International Atomic Energy Agency (IAEA). A memorable mission, and at times an unsettling experience, this was not as exciting as the IAEA's involvement might suggest. In fact, it was to provide some aid connected with ensuring that x-ray equipment and staffing arrangements in the hospitals were functioning safely and effectively. The IAEA has an ongoing commitment to such projects in the developing world; medical and other peaceful uses of radiation are a big, if not widely known, part of its business. Thus, on the surface, my mission looked simple and clear. But there are few things that Yemeni formalities can't render complicated.

I arrived in the capital Sana'a, the main point of entry to the country. At the time of writing its airport has, for practical purposes, been closed since circa 2015 as the country has become a battleground in which Saudi- and Iranian-led interests are engaged in a mixture of historical and geopolitical struggles. In simpler times, I encountered an unsettling absence of welcome among the uniformed migration officials at the airport. I got the impression they felt it would be better for Yemen, and for my wellbeing, if I were not admitted. This was, in some measure, due to being a westerner but being there at the bidding of a UN body also didn't help. In fairness, it should be said that I had received no training on how to cope with such problems and this, to put it mildly, was an oversight. I had similar experiences on other missions.

Eventually, with some help from the local host, the government's radiation regulatory body, I was admitted. On emerging into the chaotic arrival's hall, an engaging driver and a dodgy official, whom we will call 'Jabir Al-Shaqqaf', greeted me. Jabir did all in his power to establish himself as a precocious trainee clown. He was already familiar, as he had been conducting a mime act behind the glass screen that separated the detained passengers from the hectic area of the migration booths. Both greeted me with courtesy which, given the circumstances, was reassuring. Following a memorable 40-minute drive, they deposited me, incident free, at a hotel that announced itself as a Sheraton.

The visit started with a work-free acclimatisation weekend, and Jabir plus a helper took me on a wonderful tour of the centre city area. Sana'a is the product of an exceptionally sophisticated and richly cultured history. The city, then of about two million people, is perched 2,200 metres above sea level in an elevated mountain valley. The architecture and building style are unique, and not seen anywhere else in the world. The city stretches back in time to the legendary Queen of Sheba (500-600 BC). Beside it, even the most ancient of western cities are newcomers. On the tour, I became acutely aware that there were few if any westerners in the city. I don't recall seeing a single one as we walked about the central area. I gradually became conscious of attracting more attention than was comfortable. In addition, I had started to feel unwell, which exacerbated the unease of so obviously not belonging.

After a few hours, we had refreshments in a café – sweet mint tea in the Arab style with honeyed sweetmeats. Both delicious and refreshing but sticky, and a deglutinating wash was required, once finished. A feature of many restaurants and cafes is a washroom separate from the toilets, as it is customary to eat without cutlery in a fashion that almost requires total immersion once the meal is finished. It was good to be able to clean up without visiting the toilets, which could have been challenging.

Throughout the tour we came across several beautiful mosques but passed them by. Toward the end of the morning, Jabir enquired if I would like to see inside one of them.

'Yes,' I replied eagerly.

We approached one, and at the entrance to its courtyard both minders paused and consulted with each other in Arabic. Then the helper said to me: 'Wait here and we will arrange it for you.'

They both vanished through the opening in the wall into the courtyard. I was left alone on the bustling street, and subject to endless stares that were far from reassuring. Time passed, five minutes, 10 minutes and more; my unease increased and fear of being abandoned began to assert itself. However, I need not have feared; both eventually returned, sullen and accompanied by a heavily armed soldier. They explained that it was not permissible to enter, and the soldier was there to ensure we didn't try to slip in. Both guides were deflated; I was disappointed, and they dropped me back to the Sheraton.

The driver collected me early on the first working morning. Traffic was heavy and we inched from street to street. We passed back and forth over well-constructed bridges spanning a dried-up riverbed. It was there to cope with occasional torrential rain that would otherwise cause flooding. At one point, the driver pulled rapidly across the road into a side street. We travelled some hundreds of meters and eventually came alongside a wall flanking the river. The driver headed for a gap in the wall, which gave onto a slipway leading down into the riverbed, and we were off at speed for several miles, unchallenged by traffic, traffic lights or pedestrians. Anxiety asserted itself and memories of the Kuwaiti trip through the desert night flashed back. But I steadied myself hoping this was just an exercise in avoiding traffic jams. After a few kilometres, we left the riverbed and within minutes reached our destination: the offices of the Yemeni Radiation Regulator.

On entry, the Head of Section greeted me, and we moved to a large room upstairs. His desk was at one end and I was seated with Jabir, the clown, at the other. The Head explained that Jabir would be my minder for the duration; my heart sank. The seating arrangements in the room consisted of sofas along the side walls to the left and right of the Head of Section's desk. About ten people were seated, five on each side. Most were women in full burqa: large black tents, leaving only hands and eyes visible. A few men were dressed in casual western clothing, even though the Head wore a suit.

Courtesies were exchanged, and very quickly it became apparent that a one-week taught course on various medical-related issues was expected from me. Also, I was told that about 30 people including doctors, regulators and technical staff were waiting downstairs for the course to start. I was taken aback as my instructions from the IAEA were to review, over about a two-week period, practices on site in hospitals with regulators and hospital staff and help them, where possible, to improve safety and efficacy. Naturally, I didn't have a course prepared, but it was difficult to argue with the presence of 30 people downstairs. All dressed up and nowhere to go. And, notwithstanding the formalities of the situation, I knew that there was plenty of material on my laptop that could be adapted and presented as a course without great difficulty. I played for time to focus, and quickly realised that the course was a real opportunity to present the message and approaches we were anxious to explore with practitioners in Yemen.

It also became apparent that those in the Head of Section's room were seriously at odds with each other: half were from the Ministry of Health/University and the other half were from the regulator's office. Apparently, the latter had made a land grab for 'ownership' of the visit. The discussion continued, the factions baited each other, and provided me with thinking time. But, to compound matters, I was feeling even more nauseous than the previous day, and to this a throbbing vascular headache was added which made it difficult to think clearly. A bad start.

Eventually, having worked the matter through, we went downstairs to meet the 30 people. I proposed to them that we would have a series of lectures early each morning, and for the second half of the morning, until lunchtime, we would visit a different hospital or do practical demonstrations each day. During this I would have the opportunity to see what practice was like. Once this was accepted, the Head slipped out of the room, not to be seen again until a competitive dinner at the end of the visit. After a coffee break, we started and I devoted the rest of the morning to a couple of lectures and some good discussion followed.

By about 1.30 pm the group was getting restless, and I noticed that, waiting at the back, the driver and Jabir were decidedly edgy. It was time to wrap up and go home. The group dispersed and on approaching the driver, I noticed a large bulge in his right cheek, which he refreshed from time to time with green leaves, known locally as *quat (*also as *khat* or *chat).*[1] He had morphed from his normal silent, passive self and had become garrulous, agitated and more than a little high. This was the thing to do in the afternoon, once the workday was over. His driving skills had worsened dramatically from an almost respectable C⁻ and would have merited 12 penalty points in one go in Ireland.

---

1 *Quat* is used as a stimulant and is a controlled substance in many countries. In communities where the plant is native, *quat* chewing dates back thousands of years.

∞   ∞   ∞

The turf battle between the competing groups continued, and whenever we met silent hostility filled the room. I was familiar with this type of divide, which in a less severe form is also part of the Irish radiation regulatory system. Both sides manifested distrust, some animosity and an absence of expertise in the area they were trying to ensure their opponents didn't gain a foothold in. On balance, the medical side seemed more genuinely interested in learning something. A university member of that group was the only person with a clear idea of what was necessary in terms of local upskilling. I eventually formed a good working relationship with him.

On the other hand, although Jabir belonged to the regulatory group, and could not articulate what his inspectorate needed, the chance of success in the mission depended entirely on his support. This was a real problem as he had little interest in discussion if the medical group was not excluded. The early discussions consisted of suggestions from the medical group for various useful initiatives, followed by a counterbid from Jabir and his allies to the effect that these should be deferred until the regulators could teach them throughout the country.

The fact that all the women were in full burqa was unexpected and proved to be very unsettling, although I had a plenty of experience of working with Arab groups of both sexes. It became clear that it gave enormous advantage to the women. They could scrutinise the body language and demeanour of male colleagues without the normal restrictions on intense visual interrogation. I concluded that their attitude was both hostile and mocking. They tended to state their positions vis-à-vis male colleagues in a manner that lacked civility and was sometimes threatening. The only clue to what they were thinking was in the hands. When visible, the language of the hands was clear and reliable, much more so than their voices. Their eyes, often not fully visible, could only sometimes be observed, due to the shade in the poorly lit room. It was a deeply unpleasant experience, and I resolved never to be caught in such a situation again.

∞　∞　∞

My presence in Yemen was part of a wider project involving aid to developing countries, and such projects usually come with conditions. In this case, one of the conditions was that Yemen would introduce formal regulations on the use of radiation in various sectors, including medicine. I had been instructed to meet the Deputy Minister for Health (in Ireland, this would be the Secretary General of the government department) to see how the regulations were progressing. A meeting was arranged through the hosting factions for Wednesday at 12 noon. I had expected to go alone or, at most, with one person from the regulator's office. However, when teaching finished on Wednesday, the entire group assembled in the carpark and decided they would accompany me. Both sides had strong, competing vested interests in potential legislation. Trying to extract fists from the metaphorical sweet jar could prove dangerous. I was still nauseous, lightheaded and didn't have the energy for resistance.

We arrived early at the Deputy Minister's office, situated on an upper floor in a fine modern building. It was busy with lots of bustle and much of the floor was a large open space, on the scale of a parish hall, serving as a huge anteroom to the Deputy Minister's office. Of the hundred or so occupants, some were seated and some were strutting back and forth chatting in an animated fashion. Others were clearly bored and just waiting to gain admission. The women were full bur-qa'ed, some of the men dressed in western clothes and some wore the traditional Yemeni long flowing robe. This was usu-ally gathered by a sash at the waist, which also accommodated an elaborately decorated curved dagger, whose function was more than decorative.

The appointed time came and went, and the crowd grad-ually thinned, but we were not moving up the nonexistent queue. The call to prayer came around 1.00 pm and everybody vanished, returned about five minutes later, and the wait resumed. By 1.30 pm much of our delegation had become restless. This was the latest they would normally work, and domestic obligations began to loom. A senior person was dispatched to get the story. He returned almost immediately with apologies, and the news that the Deputy Minister had deferred our meeting until 2.30 pm the following afternoon, Thursday. The message was clear, he didn't like the size of the delegation and was maximally inconveniencing it by moving the meeting to Thursday afternoon, part of their weekend – the day before the weekly Muslim holy day, Friday.

∞ ∞ ∞

Amid much grumbling about practical family ar-range-ments, the lectures the following morning ground to a halt just before the lunchtime call to prayer. After some refreshments, a much-diminished group departed for the Deputy Minister's office and arrived in good time. What a dif-ference: the large anteroom was deserted, and we were shown straight into the office, a large functional modern space. It was furnished both as a personal office and as a meeting room with a dark, hardwood, polished conference table in the centre. The Deputy Minister rose and greeted us warmly; it was clear he was a cultivated, courteous man capable of great charm.

The meeting started with the usual greetings and small talk and elaborate enquiries after family and friends. Both factions briefed the Deputy Minister on their hopes and ambitions for new regulations. He listened with courtesy and interest, and I suspect instantly expunged all that was said from his mind. Eventually, he turned to me.

'Dr Malone,' he said, 'of course, you are most welcome here, and we are happy that the IAEA and its parent the UN continues to support our efforts to manage radiation on all fronts in Yemen. How have you found things since you arrived?'

'Well,' I responded, 'it's early days, but there is obviously great enthusiasm among the staff of the regulator and your own ministry to acquire skills in the area. We have a large eager group at lectures every morning. Later each day we visit hospitals and clinics and conduct demonstrations and tests, which I'll report on at the end of the visit.'

I had, in fact, come upon several somewhat alarming practices, but thought it better to leave them to a formal report.

'Excellent,' he replied. 'Of course, you will be aware we have very strong safety measures in place to protect the public. Did you know we have 25 soldiers assigned to protect the radiotherapy centre? How many soldiers have you devoted to this in Ireland?' I was shocked. The type of safety we were talking about relied on good, well-understood scientific and medical practices, not on military might. The idea of 25 soldiers outside any part of an Irish hospital was unthinkable.

'None, Minister,' I sheepishly replied. 'Our system of enforcement relies on well trained medical and technical staff and an effective inspectorate.' His demeanour became more serious.

After a pause, I continued. 'It won't be a surprise to you that the IAEA would like to hear of your progress with establishing regulations.'

We both paused. He was deciding something and reached down to the right-hand drawer of his desk. In one smooth action, he opened the drawer, removed a 50-page A4 document from it and placed it on the table.

'The regulations have been drafted,' he said, 'and the Minister for Health had them approved by the Council of State. We now have the law the UN and the IAEA expect us to have. Would you like to look through it?' he asked and he edged the document across the table towards me with his pen. I lifted the document.

A buzz of shock, excitement and confusion ran through the room. Both factions were equally perplexed and angry. An irritable discussion followed on how the law was drafted, by whom and when would it be implemented. The Deputy Minister batted these unwelcome intrusions away like flies. Meanwhile, the dispute gave me time to look through the document. On a quick scan, it addressed all the relevant issues. I placed it back on the table and the Deputy Minister skilfully retrieved it, returned it to its drawer, and despite protests it stayed there and nobody from either faction got sight of it. He then quickly drew the meeting to a close and reminded me that I should advise the IAEA et al. of the Yemeni progress in enacting legislation. I doubt if the document ever left the drawer again, except possibly to be filed in a large circular filing device on the floor. I was overcome with amusement and wonder at his mixture of skill, charm and nerve. Throughout the meeting, I continued to feel lightheaded, dizzy and nauseous, so was glad when it concluded. The prospect of slipping back to the hotel and away from the circus appealed.

Both factions were furious, and for a while it appeared the slight might unite them. But even before we left the carpark, they had reassumed their adversarial roles and were threatening each other with bitter reprisals should either group gain an upper hand. These events established patterns that persisted for the rest of the visit. Then, all departed quickly, and I was left alone with the driver who, by now, had a large bulge in his right cheek. It was 3.30 in the afternoon, and he had been chewing *quat* since 1.30 pm. The trip to the hotel was brisk and memorable.

The mystery of constant nausea and severe headaches was solved in an unlikely way later that afternoon. I was sitting in the hotel lobby after lunch working on a laptop on something that required Wi-Fi. The hotel had a Wi-Fi pass system based on per-hour charges. My pass ran out and I went to renew it at reception, which was staffed by the only non-burqa'ed woman in Yemen. I was cross-eyed from dizziness and nausea.

She looked up and enquired, 'Are you feeling okay, sir?'

'I just feel dizzy and nauseous from working on the laptop for the last couple of hours,' I replied.

'Do you often feel that way?' she responded.

'Almost all the time here,' I replied. 'It may be the pressure of the work.'

'It's not,' she replied. 'It's the altitude. This city is about 7,000 feet above sea level in old British measures. You haven't adapted – it can take up to a month, so be careful. That's why we don't have international conferences here.'

And so a mystery was solved; the anxiety was taken out of at least part of the situation, and I was able to make helpful adjustments to the daily routine. The rest of the visit continued; the protagonists wrangled with each other on every front. This even included competitive, mutually exclusive hospitality, which was both memorable and gracious. And now, I sometimes think of the individuals I came to know and work with during those days of shaded sunshine, dispute and progress, and can only hope with great uncertainty for their safety and welfare.

Chapter Nine

Vanity, Image and Reflection

*There will be, I think, ... a renewed wonder
and humility on the part of ... [those] still
capable of these basic reactions.*

– Edward Hopper

Like many people, I visit art galleries when on trips abroad. However, though pleasant, these had little impact and if the gallery had a good coffee shop it was likely to be more memorable than anything hanging on the walls. Compared with liturgy (Chapter Two) or the best of science and literature (Chapter Five) paintings didn't rate. The journey to a genuine experience of the visual arts was a long one and started with a bad reproduction of a little-known picture, *Schrödinger in the Hand of God*, by John Lighton Synge. I came across it around 1990, in a biography of the physicist Erwin Schrödinger. The painting summed up much about science, its practice, and its connection with a reflective life in general. But, at that time I didn't have the language to express this.

The dull, monochrome reproduction moved me to seek out the original. It appeared to be lost, or at least not where one might expect to find it. The search was intriguing and required persistence and commitment as well as support from the Librarian of the Dublin Institute for Advanced Studies (DIAS), Ann Goldsmith. Its disappearance arose from misgivings the artist, Synge, had about presenting it to Schrödinger who, though nominally Protestant, was attracted to eastern religions, and had little affinity with the idea of a personal God. Thus, Synge felt that offence might be taken at the anthropomorphic God image in the picture. As a fallback, he presented it to the Provost of Trinity College, A. J. McConnell, a mathematician, and a Protestant, who also didn't like it. He is believed to have displayed it in the smallest room in the large Provost's House. This ultimately contributed to its being mislaid and then lost some 30 years later.

Erwin Schrödinger, of Austrian extraction, was responsible for key insights in modern physics that combine beauty, mystery and, arguably, internal contradiction. After some resistance, his work was recognised, and he shared in the 1933 Nobel Prize in Physics. Possibly not widely known is that he worked in Ireland as a professor in the DIAS for many years, having had to flee Austria during the Nazi regime. He had a profound sense of beauty and a mystical sense of the unity of things. He had a prolific love life. This was accepted without much question in the Dublin of the time, although some questions around this topic remain to be addressed.

John Lighton Synge, the artist, was also a professor at the Institute. He was a nephew of John Millington Synge, the playwright, and defined himself as a Protestant atheist. The account of the picture below is a meditation on Synge's representation of discovery in science, particularly in physics. While acknowledging recent controversy about Schrödinger's place in the science pantheon, Synge's picture stands as an inspiring and insightful take on the scientific process. Some consideration has been given to renaming it.

The picture is approximately A5 in size, and almost completely covered in various shades of off-white, grey and blue (see second colour insert). An almost primitive, distorted representation of a face fills the right side. It is fatherly and concentrates its gaze on a large right hand, the focal point of the work. The hand clearly belongs to the same 'person' as the face, is represented in more detail, and with more emotion. Cradled in the hand is a desk set in a triangular field of light. A scientist is bent over the desk absorbed in his task and possibly smoking a pipe (suggesting Schrödinger). The background of blue-grey suggests the cosmos with hints of stars (centre), planetary systems (top left) and heavenly bodies such as the sun, earth or moon (bottom left). Throughout the cosmos the inspired flow of equations passes between God and the scientist.

One of the most striking things about the picture is its mood. It is simultaneously sombre, solemn, quiet and restful, and evokes a sense of stillness and solitude. There is stillness in the cosmos through which the inspired equations flow. There is stillness and an intimacy about both God and the man at the desk encompassed in His hand. These qualities provide the safe space in which the risky business of creativity and communication can occur and nudge the equations to unfold. Thus, the painting conveys a sense of deliberate communication against a breathtaking background that is both vast and still. Extended studies of the painting are published elsewhere.[2]

---

[2] Malone J. 2013. 'Schrödinger: Risking Mystery and Creativity in Science', *ARTS: The Journal of Arts in Religious and Theological Studies* (1) pp. 27-39. See also Malone & McEvoy *Mystery and the Culture of Science: Personal Insights for the 21ˢᵗ Century*. 2019. Cambridge Scholars. Ch 5, pp. 89-108.

A few practical remarks are in order. The equations look authentic and are of a type that would have occurred in theoretical physics at the time. I asked experts, including the then Professor of Physics and later Provost of Trinity, if they recognised the equations. The Physics Department asserted enlightened ignorance, so I published an article stating: 'It is not known if the equations are real, although they look and feel real.' Following publication, my son, David, a mathematics graduate student at the time, read the article and emailed asking me: 'Who doesn't know if the equations are real? Because I do!' He recognised them. So much for professors and experts!

I used slides of the picture many times in lectures to convey a sense of the 'numinous' in science. From the slide presentations, it became obvious that in enlarged reproductions the picture had a more forceful presence than in the smaller original. It is as though the original was a study for a larger version; the full impact of the composition requires a large scale. I learned a lot from the processes of finding, cleaning up and photographing the Synge painting. And more from its composition and message. But even more important: it was my key to the world of visual art, an unexpected gift. It has been a source of endless exploration over the last few decades, with surprising connections to the contemplative and mystical, as well as to science.

In the years that followed, art became part of day-to-day life, a rewarding enthusiasm that also provided food for reflection. It began to impact on practical decisions like how to spend spare time and holidays, and even where to live and work. It at least partly accounted for a move to Vienna for some years after retirement (Chapter Six), during which I came to know and appreciate many Austrian artists including Gustav Klimt and Egon Schiele. However, we will not concentrate on these here, but instead will look at other artists and aspects of art.

In Vienna, something in the UN building began to attract my attention: institutional art which, though important in its own way, can be less than inspiring. I had some experience of this in Trinity but never reflected on it while there – more on that a little later. The Vienna UN complex houses over 150 pieces of art, generally gifted by governments and often by celebrated artists. It is a strange mix of official art, portraits of the great and the good, art designed to make a political point, craft objects revered in member states and genuine high art. Most of the portraits of former directors and other notables are uninspiring and, with one exception, are relegated to upper floors. The exception is Kofi Annan's excellent portrait, which is on the ground floor, where it shares pride of place with 30 to 50 other excellent pieces.

These pieces are presented in the contexts of both a busy workplace and institutional art. We easily miss beautiful things when they are not where we expect them to be. The story of a 2007 *Washington Post* experiment is well known. The *Post* arranged for one of the world's great musicians, Joshua Bell, to play some of Bach's outstanding pieces on a violin worth $3.5 million in a Metro station. Over 1,000 people passed by, only six paused, and nobody applauded. While working at the UN's Vienna Headquarters in Vienna, I and many others behaved like this. Every day, we passed by without pausing to look at exceptional art works.

The IAEA/UN work practice had an unusual feature. Most offices had an open door policy, and one was free to drop into colleagues for casual discussions. However, at lunchtime people generally closed the door and had a nap, talked to their partners on the phone, did online shopping or were otherwise disengaged. So out of boredom, at lunchtime, I took to walking the long corridors, noting and trying to identify each artwork and why it was there. A few are introduced here that effectively combine artistic expression with a nuclear inspiration – an unlikely combination.

Man after the Hydrogen Bomb by Andre Verlon recalls Munch's *The Scream* which appears everywhere from Andy Warhol to *The Simpsons*. Verlon's work dives deep behind the unsettling threats and hopes of the early nuclear era. His concerns are spiked with a cheeky Austrian sense of *we've been through all this before and perhaps we'll survive*. Many of the other works from the early years of the collection reflect the post-WWII/Cold War mood. They were gifts from governments (especially the Austrian government) around the time the building was commissioned in 1979/80.

An extraordinary and unexpectedly hopeful piece is a large dark sculpture, so poorly lit that it might be removed without being noticed (see second colour insert). I passed this up to four times a day for years without recognising what it is. Close inspection proved rewarding. It is a massive, heavy, tough looking man that might have been inspired by the Incredible Hulk. He is wearing a kaftan-like garment gathered at the waist. His upper body and head are surrounded by birds, creating a forbidding image reminiscent of Hitchcock's film. Eventually, cleaning a dust-encrusted metal tag on the plinth revealed that the statue is called *St Francis and the Birds* and was created by German sculptor Helmar Hillebrand. It was a gift from the Holy See (the Vatican), presented in 1980 by the then Secretary of State, Cardinal Casaroli, on behalf of the late Pope, now Saint, John Paul II. Checking IAEA board records reveals that its poor position and lighting owe to differences of opinion on where it should be placed. In this case the 'buildings department' won.

One must assume the Vatican had a point to make in such an unusual gift. And it had: around 1980 the Pope made several interventions in the ecological crisis. Among these was naming St Francis of Assisi as the Patron Saint of Ecology. This defines the context of the gift: recognition that protecting nature will require a tough and determined approach. The statue is a forceful affirmation of the challenge inherent in the mission of the IAEA, which simply stated is the prevention of the harmful impacts of nuclear proliferation and promoting peaceful uses of nuclear sciences. Beautiful, perhaps not. Impressive and provocative, yes. And a vivid reminder of what is expected from a UN agency.

Many of the works open the mind and/or lift the spirit. My personal favourite is a wonderful work, *Cantico de Synnaquir*, by Antonio Máro. This was presented by the government of Peru in 1998. It is an abstract work characteristic of the artist. His paintings and ceramic/glass objects are colourful, beautiful, nonfigurative and create a mood that lifts the spirit.

The drama continues in a large, white stone block, *Woman Free*, by a member of the Churchill family, Edwina Sandys. It is both forceful and self-explanatory. Beside it a recent Iranian gift, *The Pavilion of Scholars*, leaves little doubt on the respect due to older civilisations and our indebtedness to them. The collection is rich in reassuring, calming and beautiful works that would enhance any building. For example, Manuel Dalao Baldemor's wonderful painting *Pasasalamat (Thanksgiving)* would enhance any building. His folk art style celebrates the traditions of his hometown in the Phillipines, and his designs have sold over a million greeting cards for UNICEF.

These treasures are accessible to all working in or visiting the building as they go to meetings, the cafeteria, the bank, the post office or even step outside for a smoke. However, when I was there, they were relatively unknown to staff as there was no inventory or commentary to help identify the works and excavate meaning. I tried to gain attention for the collection through an article written for a good quality in-house bulletin. Initially, I pressed the editor to publish something on it, and he declined, expressing doubt that it would attract any interest. I challenged him to read the 1,000 words I would write on it and see if he found it interesting. He accepted the challenge. I wrote the piece, he found it interesting and agreed to publish it. And then Fukushima happened and there was no space for anything except related articles. By the time that had died down, I had moved on, the editor had moved on, and the project lost momentum.

The IAEA is a special place and, like a secular cathedral, it carries much of the hope of humanity for a future in which it will not destroy itself. Visitors responded warmly to artwork tours I organised there during conferences from 2010 to 2016. I found endless hours of enjoyment, discovery and insight there that transformed otherwise boring lunchtimes into periods of discovery. I hope the institution will take the steps to open the work up to the thousands who pass it every year.

Of course, the UN also has uninspiring institutional art and it is not the only place that does. I spent several years in an office in Trinity College that held more than its share of bad art. And while there are some great pieces, particularly in its public spaces, the college provided a secure home for some less-than-appealing art. The dean's office in the School of Medicine used to be a fine room in the old chemistry building. The school itself was dispersed in the teaching hospitals so this was a neutral place where the perennial conflicts between the warring factions in the hospitals and the college could be brought together. It was attractive and formally decorated in a traditional manner. The walls carried portraits of notables from centuries past and the more recent deans. The earlier paintings, of mixed quality, were richly framed and lent gravitas to the room. The portraits from the last hundred years are smaller, generally head-and-shoulders images.

My clearest recollection is a portrait of one of the six deans from the twenty plus years I was directly involved in college affairs: Professor John Bonnar by Robert Ballagh. John was an obstetrician with the decisiveness one associates with surgeons. He had piercing eyes and an unnerving, focused gaze, even when confusing matters were being discussed. I recall the Master of the Rotunda declaring that John's first name must be Professor. The artist faithfully captured this and his decisiveness. When I occupied the office, John's portrait was in my line of vision from the desk. I found it unsettling and eventually had it moved to another location in the room.

Ian Temperley (RIP) was dean immediately after John Bonnar and Dermot Hourihane (RIP) was immediately before him. Both were from the laboratory side of medicine and made important contributions. Ian was from haematology and pioneered bone marrow transplantation and treatment of haemophilia. Dermot was from histopathology and we owe the large, integrated, modern laboratory at St James's Hospital to him. On the other hand, we owe both of their portraits to the same miscreant. They are appalling, poor likenesses and both look disreputable, as though they had spent a long time in Dorian Gray's attic.

The end of Ian's career was troubled by the blood scandals, and he spent much of the last active decade of his life searching through records in the various hospitals he served in to help answer the charges that were levelled against him. At the end, the judge in the Lindsay tribunal paid warm tribute to him in respect of his professionalism, his bravery, his candour and his contributions to the tribunal. I'm glad none of his adversaries found the portrait in the dean's office as it may have been used to damage him further. The decent thing to do with both of these portraits would be to remove them and have them replaced by something more worthy of the individuals involved. Not doing so while I was dean is one of my few regrets.

James McCormick (RIP), another exceptional figure, found himself dean. His portrait has the merit of being bland, but in a strange way it is true to him, which can only be good. He was a reflective character with a philosophical bent. He was a great source of aphorisms which could easily be coaxed from him. For example, he had little time for health education puritans and did not believe in giving people a lot of advice about drink and related matters. He used to say: 'The purpose of medicine is not to make men virtuous, rather it is to comfort them in dealing with the consequences of their excesses.' A sentiment that might be worth drawing to the attention of some of the doctors I've sat across the table from.

The first piece of art I commissioned for the college was the portrait of Davis Coakley, who was dean immediately before me (1993-1999). We had a good working relationship and had laboured on many initiatives together, often involving attempts to improve and recast the relationship between the college and the major teaching hospitals. The faculty administrator suggested an artist, and some months later the completed portrait was delivered. Davis found it acceptable, and although I was uneasy about it, we accepted it and it now hangs with the other portraits in the series in the new faculty office in the Biomedical Sciences building in Pearse Street. With hindsight, I feel that it misses the firmness of resolve that is a feature of Davis's character, and somehow suggests he is a pushover and easy to please. Nothing is farther from the truth.

One of the more remarkable pieces of public art in Trinity is *Sfera con Sfera* (Sphere within a Sphere) by Arnoldo Pomodoro. It is a stunning piece sitting outdoors in the area between the old Long Room and the newer Berkley Libraries. It is a large, polished, bronze globe, capable of rotating on its axis. It has great solidity and is an authentic statement about the world in all its fractured complexity. Other versions of *Sfera* can be seen outside the UN building in New York, in the Vatican and elsewhere. I use slides of it as a signature image for the university and it also appears on the cover of a book I published on ethics issues. Pomodoro was more than generous in allowing me to use it. Both the space in which it is placed and the piece itself are magnets for visitors. Trying to photograph it on a beautiful summer day was a pointless task, as there were too many visitors. Later in the evening there were still visitors and attempts to photograph it were interrupted by an officious college security man. But we persisted, and once he was out of sight we got the photographs needed for the book cover.

In *Sfera* and the Schrödinger picture, the artists decisively expose an aspect of reality to us – sometimes before we know it is happening and almost in spite of ourselves. This is one of the most direct and immediate connections to truth we can experience. Today, the trusted sources of such revelatory experiences are the arts and literature. Sometimes, perhaps, they are trusted even more than they deserve. The trust is there because we know this is an important part of what art is about. It relies on the artist being open to the truth, and of course on the observer (or reader) being open to receiving it. Mystical experience also relies on this openness to the truth.

Religion should also bring us into contact with truth. However, today it seems to have let us down, and not just because of the sex scandals. There have been real failures of scholarship rooted in an abuse of authority (including infallibility) that have distanced the churches from great swathes of truth. Distrust of religion carries a whiff of decay that the public, even those still sympathetic to religion, don't quite know how to deal with. Like a bad case of body odour or halitosis, it is often just politely ignored. Some years ago, during an earlier humanitarian crisis in Myanmar, the generals would only allow foreign aid to be distributed through the machinery provided by *their* government. Thus, the aid acquired a whiff of the generals. Likewise, consistent neglect and misreading of truth by the churches carries something like the corrupted stench of Myanmar and its generals.

The opportunity to commission another piece by Pomodoro arose in connection with the development of the Trinity Centre for Health Sciences at St James's Hospital. *The Shield* is a remarkable work that was initially expected to be attached to the upper level of the planned two-storey building, just facing the entrance gate to the hospital. When permission for a higher structure was secured, this plan was abandoned, and it is now displayed in the entrance foyer. The funding arrangements were precarious and required a cat-and-mouse game of smoke and mirrors to protect the allocation for the artwork from the demands of the faculty for more mundane items. Eventually, with the help of the administrator, the funds were committed in a way that did not allow them be diverted. I sometimes privately celebrate this small but important antidemocratic success. In future, I suspect many people may visit the building just to see Pomodoro's work and enjoy it more than anything else that happens in this now busy and successful centre. A fine set of relief prints by Pomodoro was associated with this acquisition and now hangs in the Trinity Centre at Tallaght Hospital after a perilous period in storage in the college. Several other works were also purchased and can be seen throughout the faculty buildings.

About a year after retiring, the incoming dean Derry Shanley phoned and asked if I was willing to have a portrait done. I enquired if he had an artist in mind and he suggested one that did his own portrait, which could be seen on the top floor of the Dental Hospital. I went and looked: the artist had captured a good likeness of Derry. However, the full length oil painting also gave free rein to a shifty, evasive quality that most of those familiar with Derry will recognise. By coincidence, a similar large portrait of Donald Weir, the retired Professor of Medicine, had appeared in the Trinity Centre in St James's Hospital. Both are lavish, and I suspect should carry an acknowledgment to the sponsors. Both are unsympathetic, although the subjects seemed unaware of this. I have no doubt about Derry's, though some people, whose opinion is worth listening to, disagree about Donald's.

In view of this, I declined Derry's proposal, but suggested a friend and artist, Des Hickey, who would not wield his brush with malice. Derry agreed and the project proceeded. Conversations with Des during sittings were interesting. At one stage he asked if there was anything I would like to suggest. All the representations in the faculty office were solemn and serious, so I felt one with a smile would be a welcome change. This provoked a long discussion about teeth and how they can ruin a portrait, so he settled for a glimmer of a smile. I did not see the portrait as it progressed, but when all was revealed it seemed, to my eye at least, to be good.

Later, my unwillingness to risk a potentially unsympathetic portrait began to bother me, and I also wondered if a friend had been placed in a compromising situation. After all, a portrait should have something of truth, warts and all. However, some special considerations arise with end-of-term portraits in formal institutional settings. There is something of the obituary about them. We tend not to speak ill of the 'dead', that is, those who have no opportunity to reply. Faced with this, and the worryingly unsympathetic representations of colleagues, for good or ill, I cared enough to try to avoid it.

∞   ∞   ∞

Having spent so much time exploring 'official' art, it is time to have a look at the real thing. Sometimes official art is the real thing, but it may be just decorative, or flattering, or even mischievous. However, the real thing is different and takes us somewhere we might not otherwise go. I have been fascinated, horrified and delighted by some of the great modern artists. There are so many, including Edward Hopper,

Gustav Klimt, Egon Schiele, Juan Miró, Alberto Giacometti, René Magritte, Francie Bacon, Frida Kahlo, Yayoi Kusama and Sean Scully, among others. I ask your indulgence as room here allows us to explore only one, and faced with an impossible choice, I selected Edward Hopper. He speaks very directly to me, and also enjoys a mixture of popularity and notoriety.

Hopper's works have been dubbed 'metaphors of silence', something in short supply in today's world. Silence is not a normal subject for art, but some great works evoke it, for example, the *Mona Lisa*, Rembrandt's wonderfully contemplative *Philosopher in Meditation* and some Dutch seventeenth century quasi-domestic works such as those by Vermeer or Metsu. All of these resonate with silence and stillness. Yet the *Mona Lisa*, though silent and knowing, is, perhaps, a little judgmental. For some she creates unease.

Hopper's best known and much loved painting *Nighthawks* (1942) is widely reproduced as a poster. As part of a newfound interest in art in the mid-1990s, I went to see the original in Chicago, where I attended a radiology conference most years. *Nighthawks'* reputation was as an icon of loneliness and alienation, and visiting it was something of a box-ticking exercise. I didn't expect much, however once there was drawn to it but not as an icon of loneliness or alienation. It was compelling in a different and more winning way. Hopper said of it, '[It] seems to be the way I think of a night street. I didn't see it as particularly lonely.' He added on another occasion, 'the loneliness thing is overdone'. Later, in New York, I had a few days to kill, and went on impulse to the Whitney Museum which has a good collection of his work. I was captured by its often unfinished quality and its quiet but eloquent visual articulation of much that cannot be reduced to words. I returned many times to the Whitney and other galleries over the following days, and cemented an enduring relationship with his work. A similar relationship was established with Egon Schiele's work during visits to Vienna for equally unconnected purposes (Chapter Six).

A *New York Times* review of a Museum of Modern Art (MOMA) show of Hopper's work observed '... [it] is suffused by a meditative wit that wears its transcendent ambitions lightly'. A nuanced reading of his work suggests he has much to offer those on a personal spiritual journey. His work evokes empathy and normalises silence, solitude and mystery, none of which are explicitly celebrated in popular culture. He says, 'I am interested primarily in the vast field of experience and sensation which neither literature nor a purely plastic art deals with...' Ambitious – and he succeeds. In my experience of his work, many of his subjects are not particularly alienated. On the contrary, they are composed, appear to have an inner strength and often radiate stillness. He worked slowly; in later life, he struggled with his subjects until he had found what interested him most. Then he was ready to start painting. He was like Voltaire, who remarked, 'My book is finished; all I have to do is write it'.

Brian O'Doherty, an Irish friend of Hopper's, left one of the few video portraits of him, and felt, 'he achieved a neutrality that made his pictures available to numerous readings, depending on the observer's capacities'. He is the Vermeer of the twentieth century and is one of those special artists who paints aspects of life his predecessors missed. His influence on film director Alfred Hitchcock and the TV series *Mad Men* is beyond question.

The women and men in Hopper's scenes are often relatively self-contained. They can appear physically slight but have an inner strength that sustains them in the face of the brutality of urban landscapes. As often as not, they are quiet and unimpressed, a picture that is surprisingly consistent with the wisdom literature of some religions, although he never explicitly references this. His works have a calming effect, and what is left unsaid suggests the inner strength of a deep personal secular spirituality. It is almost as though he is discovering this *de novo* for himself.

Hopper painted the part beyond words that we can't otherwise reach. He validated silence, solitude and a meditative poise as part of living. Of course, there are many other works, many more artists, and endless other inspiring themes that it would be nice to visit. But they are tales for another day.

Chapter Ten

Calls for Help: The Bishop,
a Philanthropist and the Camino

To err is human, to forgive, divine.

– Alexander Pope

An afternoon in the office always left me feeling congested, blocked sinuses –probably caused by the carpet. It
had been a difficult afternoon with multiple meetings, more
than its share of conflict, and bruising encounters with alarming, big, intelligent egos. I was glad to leave. Outside the air
was welcoming, autumn chilly, and a relief after the overheat-
ed afternoon. I enjoyed deep satisfying breaths while walking toward the front of college. My sinuses cleared; the day's
troubles were replaced by pleasant anticipation of a solitary
evening at home. By the time I reached the Pearse Street gate,
I was only mildly irritated by the three-deep layer of socially
unacceptable parking outside the Garda station.

I eased my heavily sprung front door closed and entered the welcoming solitude. Rounding the corner into the
lounge, the flashing light on the phone caught my eye; five
messages, not uncommon before answering machines were
replaced by texts etc. Two were undemanding and personal,

two businesses requesting return calls that could wait – okay so far. I pressed play on the final one and headed for the kitchen to put on the kettle, but stopped short.

Heavy breathing, and eventually, 'Hello Jim.' It sounded like someone half asleep. A breathy pause followed and, eventually, with some difficulty, 'I'm calling from the hospice.' It sounded as though the person was heavily sedated, and possibly found moving difficult. But, from the intonation, I recognised the voice.

It was a friend I will call 'John', not intimate but close. He was in his early fifties, about five years younger than me at the time, which was around the year 2001. He was gay, not in an ostentatious way, but there was little doubt about it. A priest, he had retained boyish good looks through the years and was always well groomed, not always the case with clerics who had abandoned the traditional uniform. His job involved providing support for missionaries in the developing world, but he was discreet, and I never quite understood what he did or, indeed, how he managed his sexuality. But that is common with friends and acquaintances. He was good company, had found a way of living within the church without having his spirit or sexuality crushed, and we had a meal together with other friends three or four times a year.

Over a year prior to this, John had been diagnosed with cancer and when we last met a month or so before, he seemed stable, in high spirits, and was able to do justice to a good dinner. But a call from the hospice was a shock, ominous. Normally, he was animated, lively, but his voice was now sluggish – not his style. The message, though relatively brief was not coherent – it seemed the cancer was going to take him quickly. I replayed it and eventually I pieced together:

'Try to remember "Dermot Dwyer", an order priest we talk-ed about, who was made Archbishop of "Latville", the capital of a province in one of the new African states. He may be in trouble and needs help.' (The name of the bishop and city are also pseudonyms.)

I did indeed remember him, a big happy energetic man with a generous spirit and can-do approach. He was the type who would be in permanent trouble and well able to deal with it. John paused again – it seemed endless – eventually he made a big effort and said:

'When he was made Archbishop, I helped him fund a hostel for AIDS victims and addicts... Successful... Last year, a young man was killed or possibly died as a result of something that happened in the hostel... The man's family are angry and have issues with how the hostel was run. Dermot and the staff may be caught in the frame of the blame game.' He paused again, even the sound of the breathing ceased. He must have put the phone down. Eventually:

'He was running the place on a shoestring, but I think it was okay. Medical... addiction... management questions in-volved. Can you help him?'

John sounded exhausted and withdrawn. The phone went silent, but the line remained open. I was shocked and alarmed. How could I do anything for somebody in Latville? I didn't even know where it was on the map. Was what Dermot Dwyer was doing really okay? The religious orders took short cuts, albeit often for good causes. The heavy breathing returned, and John's now feeble voice made a final effort:

'I sent you files with all the information. Will you look af-ter it for me?'

'Of course I will,' I responded to the answering machine as though John could hear me, but thought: 'What can I do?'

John was obviously heavily sedated and possibly in the terminal phase of his illness. The message was deeply disturbing, nearly incoherent and difficult to sort out on the spot. Was he just raving, which wouldn't be unusual if he was on morphine? My mind was racing – how could I do anything for somebody I barely knew in such a remote place? What did the situation involve? Was it dangerous? And so on, question after question began to form in my mind, none of them reassuring. But it was obviously of great importance to John, and he feared his impending death would stand in the way of its being dealt with effectively. I went to the kitchen, made some tea, sat down, brooded, and resolved to meet him as soon as possible, preferably the following day. The prospect of a quiet, relaxed evening had vanished.

∞   ∞   ∞

John wasn't allowed visitors other than immediate family during the days that followed. The thought that he might be only raving began to gain traction, and I wondered if I should wait and see if the files he mentioned turned up. Once I had read them, I could chat with him. Two days after his call a collection of documents, enough to fill a big suitcase, was delivered by courier. This was too much to study immediately, and I put them aside to read at the weekend.

I retained hope of seeing John to better understand the basis for his conviction that the bishop had acted correctly and should be helped. But events intervened and he died a couple of days later. His funeral was, as one might expect, a large and disparate one, including some of his colleagues. However, it didn't seem appropriate to mention the matter to them as, right or wrong, he must have decided he could not entrust it to them. I decided not to raise the issues with any church people, other than the archbishop. He might be the only one with first-hand knowledge of the troubled situation, but he wasn't at the funeral. Nevertheless, chatting with various clerics from John's organisation, I listened carefully for clues as to what might lie behind his request. But nothing emerged, nothing at all, and I was left perplexed and unsettled.

When the crowd started to disperse, I avoided the official post-funeral reception. A nearby pub provided tea, a sandwich and an opportunity to ponder again why John had entrusted this task to me and not to his order. I thanked the waitress and left, convinced that earlier suspicions of some breach of trust remained the most likely explanation. It was at a time when we had started to hear convincing evidence that the church was more concerned about protecting its reputation and assets than it was about acting properly. I resolved to find a way forward that didn't initially involve contacting the archbishop or his order. Step one would be a detailed study of the bundle of files, and then it might be possible to make an action plan.

∞   ∞   ∞

So, what was it all about? Latville was trying to navigate its way through many inherited problems including homelessness and addiction. Out of desperation, the bishop established a basic hostel to provide shelter and support for addicts and the dispossessed, without as much supervision, medical and otherwise, as one would like if deeper pockets and more skills were available. But, on the surface, it seems much better than nothing.

A young man died at the hostel, in a situation where both violence and drugs are commonplace. Possibly an overdose of substances provided in the hostel? His family are understandably angry, find fault with the medical staff and possibly, by implication, with the bishop. They search for flaws in the arrangements at the hostel, of which inevitably there are many. Confirming earlier impressions, my friend might not have fully trusted the order to support the situation adequately. The staff and bishop were practical people motivated by charity, and might take personal risks to find workable solutions to intractable problems. Did the idea of establishing a hostel have full support from the authorities in Ireland?

John wanted to ensure the problem would be addressed in the round and that the staff and the bishop would not be pilloried for doing the best they could in an impossible situation. But I knew little of drugs, addiction, homelessness, violence and social deprivation in Latville. Eventually, I concluded that the solution would have to involve somebody with a deep knowledge of these areas who also had experience of legal and social matters.

Following guarded discussion with medical and legal colleagues, the ideal person, Pat Plunkett, came to mind almost unbidden. He is a bright, colourful character, a relatively formal dresser, often sporting a bow tie. He is small in stature with a well-trimmed beard, a ready smile, and is quick to engage in conversation often in a deliberative style, but not without humour. At that time, Pat was the Consultant in charge of Emergency Medicine in St James's Hospital where, as often as not, he sported scrubs and a jacket. St James's Emergency Department sees the best and worst of city life, including the problems arising from drug and alcohol abuse. He has a wide experience of medico-legal problems and the worst that can happen when everything goes wrong. Equally important, he was experienced in court proceedings, something that many would find intimidating.

Pat had been a member of the hospital board and chairman of its medical board over a long period, giving him an appreciation of institutional accountability and how to live with it when resources did not match the problems. His experience in the emergency department led him to become the conscience of the hospital board when it had to grapple with insoluble problems. I got to know him over time, and he had helped me with personal medical issues, always with courtesy and usually effectively. However, as was common in the hospital, I had no idea of his religious affiliations (if any) but was confident that he would be fair and bring experience moderated by wisdom to the situation.

So, I approached him promptly but with some trepidation – it was a big ask. He agreed to take a preliminary look at the bulky files and assess the situation. Within a few days, he agreed that it needed a robust intervention, and said he would look favourably on getting involved. For the first time since receiving the phone message, it looked as though a good outcome might be possible.

With Pat on board, and an authoritative judgment on the contents of the files, I felt an approach to the order would be possible without risking peremptory dismissal. A little research identified its head office in Ireland and that a priest we will refer to as 'Father Kevin' was the person in charge of day-to-day business. By coincidence, I had met him briefly on a social occasion a few years earlier. On that occasion, he presented a smooth, polished front with some charm and an underlying seriousness. A call with suitable introductions was arranged and the following conversation ensued:

'Hello!' he said, 'Father Kevin speaking.'

'Father Kevin,' I responded. 'We met a few years ago at –. My condolences on the loss of John Kelly. He was too young to die – and at the end went very quickly.'

'Yes,' he replied. 'Far too young, only 55.' And then silence.

'A few days before he died, he sent a large file to me connected with a problem in Latville. He asked that I read it and take whatever measures necessary to deal with the problems involved, particularly if they put the staff or Archbishop Dwyer at risk.'

'Yes,' he responded, and again silence followed. Obviously, this was not a welcome call. I expected that, at this stage, he might be curious about the contents of the file, but no, only frosty silence.

'I read the file carefully. And feel some of the hostel staff, and indirectly the bishop, may be exposed. They need expert evaluation of all the circumstances of the situation that takes account of what they have been trying to achieve.'

'I see,' he responded, and an intimidating silence ensued.

It seemed he resented the intrusion and was mounting a high horse with the intention of staying up there. I tried moving away from the contents of the file and explained how it had come to me, and that John had been a trusted friend over an extended period.

'In the circumstances, there was little choice other than to try to address the problems John raised, including the management of the centre, the death of the young man, and the right and wrong ways of dealing with such issues in the context of Latville. I found a person with the right profile, and deep relevant experience, who is willing to help.'

'Okay,' he responded without enthusiasm.

'Would you like him to contact you, so that you can make arrangements to try to address things properly?' I asked.

'Hmph. Okay, we really don't have a choice, do we?'

The conversation moved to a conclusion and arrangements for Pat to contact Father Kevin were agreed. I was disturbed by the calculated coolness and the lack of engagement, which suggested both prior knowledge and a hope that the problem would just go away. The lack of reciprocity was understandable at one level, but was also irritating and invited disengagement. However, my commitment to John countered this and made it necessary to continue.

∞   ∞   ∞

This ended my involvement with an emerging, exciting story. The order stepped up to the plate and Pat Plunkett got involved and headed for Latville. After he returned, I met him socially and was reassured the situation had been resolved. The reality on the ground was that a religious sister was most exposed. She, a retired doctor, was supervising detoxification at the centre. An inmate/patient had died from an overdose, allegedly due to improper use of methadone. The Archbishop was at less risk than John's reports suggested. However, he was concerned that there might be financial claims against the diocese and a case against the sister that might lead to criminal proceedings and conviction.

The prosecutor took an aggressive approach supported by a doctor who was providing competing rapid detoxification services in the private sector. Once Pat was in the witness box, the prosecutor commented:

'Well, Doctor Plunkett, I appreciate you have great experience with heroin.'

'Excuse me!' Pat replied. 'My only experience is of dealing with those who use heroin – I have no personal experience of the drug itself.'

The Magistrate/Coroner found it difficult to keep a straight face. In addition, an unsatisfactory post-mortem demonstrated the presence in the deceased of drugs, which were unavailable in the centre, but which had probably been tossed over the fence. The pathologist and the investigating prosecutor had missed this. The verdict was death by misadventure, with no blame attaching to the sister or the centre.

The hostel could continue. The Archbishop, the sister and staff were no longer at risk. A good outcome and I think John would be happy. I wonder to what extent Pat's expertise and contribution are, in retrospect, known or appreciated in the diocese. They were given at short notice and, as I later became aware, to a denomination to which he did not belong. I wasn't surprised as he was always incisive, generous and fair. As you will see later in this chapter, through an unusual coincidence, I was able to respond in kind to Pat's generosity many years afterwards.

Not all requests for help to professors involve missionaries, bishops and remote African states. Most are local and include worthy, occasionally eccentric, projects. Most need expertise and/or some research that is the business of universities (Chapter Four). Inevitably students are among those needing help. But the great and the good, such as politicians and the CEOs of large organisations, also often have intractable problems that they just can't resolve. Interested academics, aware of the world they live in – and most are – often spend time and energy on such conundrums, the more difficult the better. A few examples follow.

∞   ∞   ∞

On a cold spring morning early in the new century, I walked briskly across the Trinity front square, anxious to reach the distant warmth of the medical school office. A colleague, Pat Wall, was approaching from the nearby arts block; he hailed me, and I stopped. As usual, he was unhurried, and once greetings were exchanged, he enquired:

'Would anybody from the medical school be willing to meet a politically affiliated person with a worthwhile project?'

'That would depend on the affiliation, the person and the project. But hopefully we wouldn't be found wanting,' I replied.

'Well,' he said, 'the affiliation, it won't surprise you – is Fianna Fáil. I can vouch for the project, it's impressive and, if it comes off, it will have a big impact. The person is not a politician but has a high profile as an independent minded mover and shaker. I can't say more than that without a commitment from somebody to meet him.'

I paused for a few moments and enquired, 'Do you have anybody in mind?'

'No,' he replied. 'As long as they know how the system here works. You'd be okay yourself. But you may not have the time or the inclination. Anybody competent would do, if they can navigate the college system.'

'And,' he added after a pause, 'a patronising attitude, or a *Trinity* accent won't survive for five minutes in this case.'

We talked a little more around accents, pretentious London teaching hospital consultants of the *Carry On Doctor* variety and the initiative, which seemed intriguing. Not being able to resist a heady mixture of curiosity and opportunity, I agreed to meet the mystery man. After all, Pat wasn't given to wasting one's time or leading one astray. Some weeks later, a call came through to the dean's office in the Medical School and a meeting was arranged for about 8.00 am with a highly successful, independent-minded lawyer and businessman, and well known supporter of the party then in government, whom we will refer to as 'Mark Grey'.

∞   ∞   ∞

At the designated hour, I was well established in the office, a large high-ceilinged room with a sense of history. The receptionist phoned to say that Mark Grey and entourage had arrived and were waiting. She showed them in. The group consisted of about half dozen plan-laden and suited men, all deferential to their leader. I greeted all and directed them to the conference table in the middle of the room. Grey was a tall, well-built man in middle years, and wore a light grey suit, had well-coiffed white hair and piercing blue eyes. He explained the role of each of his team and then looked at me squarely and asked:

'Have you ever heard of the Little Flower?'

'Of course,' I replied, taking my place at the head of the table. 'You mean St Theresa of Lisieux?' I am of a generation that would have heard of the Little Flower. She was a Carmelite mystic, noted for her simplicity. She died young and less than five years before this conversation was declared one of only four female Doctors of the Catholic Church.

'Well, I've great devotion to the Little Flower,' he replied, and his gaze softened a little. 'Her parents, Louis and Zelie Martin, were wonderful people, but suffered greatly in the final stages of their lives. That's why I'm here – I want to build a hospice in their memory.'

He sat to my left and one by one he got his acolytes to present details of the architecture, engineering, physical and medical aspects, staffing and financial modelling for the creation of a new hospice on the site of a former convent. Apparently, it would be financed by building apartments on part of the site, selling them and using the surplus to finance the hospice. A measure of the quality and attention to detail was in the way patient's rooms were planned to face on to a beautiful garden. Nothing was left to chance. The garden design was entered competitively at Chelsea Flower Show, won in its category, and featured in many TV and press reports at the time. All aspects of the plans were rigorous, impressive and remarkably complete. As the presentations went on, it was difficult to imagine what Mark might want from the university. So I interjected:

'How can the university help?' His gaze refocused and combined with that in the portrait of one of my predecessors also to the left (Chapter Nine).

He replied: 'I'm determined that this will be the best hospice in the country and am told the way to achieve this is by making sure the medical director has a seat in a university.'

I was puzzled, fumbled a response, and asked him to expand. What did he mean by seat in the university? Did he want membership of the board or council of the university or one of the teaching hospitals? Nothing he said clarified the matter, but he continued and talked around ideas about leadership in the hospice movement, medicine, and training new people in the field. And then suddenly, the penny dropped, and I realised that what he meant by a 'seat in a university' was a professorship – a chair.

He had researched it well and his strategy was correct. The meeting moved quickly and decisively to a conclusion. I agreed to do what I could to facilitate establishment of a professorship and started thinking about how to persuade the faculty it would be a good idea. The project materialised, along the lines envisaged, in the following years. I had the privilege of visiting it on several occasions during the construction phase.

But, following my time, it appears that somebody dropped the ball and the professorship was established in another university.

∞   ∞   ∞

We began to disengage and drifted into the chit-chat that precedes the end of a meeting.

'Have you abandoned the law?' I asked.

'More or less,' he replied. 'At present, business and all that goes with it is completely absorbing. For example, I spent yesterday in London trying to resolve problems. It wasn't easy but had to be done.'

'Do you miss the law? You were a powerful advocate for the last hour and a half.'

'Of course,' he said. 'But I still have two clients I look after, out of duty or loyalty.'

'Would it be rude to enquire who they are?' I asked.

He paused and named a prominent buiness man and a local bishop.

Both were public figures in trouble at the time. And with that he left the office and departed, unhurried, at 9.30 am. This happened about 20 years ago and stands out among the hundreds, if not thousands, of meetings that year.

Later that day, the TV news showed Mark's business client emerging from a tribunal which was enquiring into the financial affairs of government. During his testimony, the business man created a wonderful new verb: an individual involved had immediately *trousered* a cheque handed to him. The news report indicated it had been a long day at the tribunal and that those emerging looked tired, except for Mark Grey who still looked immaculate. He had left my office about 9.30 am, which gave him just time to walk to Dublin Castle. My bet is that he was as well prepared for the tribunal as he had been for the encounter in Trinity and that his ally, the Little Flower, accompanied him to both.

Students are at the centre of life in universities. There are endless occasions when individuals or groups need a helping hand and staff make the time to respond. Indeed, people are specifically appointed to assist students (or staff) who need support. In Trinity, every student has a tutor whose role includes being available to them when needed.

Sometimes help is needed even before they become students. For example, in the 1990s, I was approached by colleague Pat Wall (see earlier) on behalf of a school in an underprivileged area of Dublin. They had an exceptionally gifted Leaving Certificate student who was highly motivated toward doing medicine but unlikely to get the necessary points. The school was adamant that in more favourable circumstances she would be among the top performers in the country. The Trinity Access Programme (TAP) for students from underprivileged backgrounds was just beginning and had not yet had an outing in the medical school, which was generally oversubscribed with high performers. There were also endless special representations on behalf of privileged students from influential backgrounds whose parents felt they deserved a place. The only bulwark against this was to rigidly apply the points system.

We considered the merits of the case and decided to make way for this talented student, both to establish that it could be done and to respond to her individual case. However, we also had to do it in a way that did not create an avalanche of special representations or accusations of unfairly admitting a student without the points. So, we decided to interview her to establish her commitment to and interest in medicine. A member of the faculty we will refer to as 'Professor Pine' had a clinic in the prospective student's area. He arranged with colleagues to interview her. Favourable reports followed, and in due course the young woman became the first person from her area to be admitted to the Trinity Medical School. She was a trailblazer, and since then many have followed her in the TAP programme.

An exchange at a function shortly after the new student started in college gives a flavour of her attitude. A senior staff member asked:

'Did you find the interview very intimidating?'

'Not at all,' she replied. 'It wasn't in the college anyway. They arranged for it to be in Professor Pine's practice, which is not far from where I live.'

'That must have been very convenient.'

'Not really!' she replied again. 'I went to his place on the day. They have a lovely receptionist there and I asked for the professor, saying about the interview. But, the receptionist says, sez she, "sure, he's never here".'

'And what happened?'

'Well, in fairness, they'd arranged for a gang of other fellas to do it and it worked out grand. So, no one's complaining!'

The story of Emergency Medicine Consultant Pat Plunkett and the Archbishop at the beginning of this chapter had a strange sequel almost a decade and a half later. By then, Pat had been appointed CEO of St James's Hospital and facilitating the new children's hospital was top of the agenda. I was surprised that he agreed to accept the appointment, but perhaps the daily battles and chaos of the Emergency Department were good training for his new role. Unexpectedly, his appointment led to a strange reciprocal opportunity to do him a favour that, in a small way, returned his generosity in dealing with the crisis in Latville. This incident happened before the problems about the cost overruns in building the new hospital came to light.

A little background information is necessary. St James's is the most recent name given to an institution with a long and sometimes troubled history stretching back over several centuries. The name draws on historical associations with the nearby St. James's Gate, the former western entrance to the mediaeval city. It also references Guinness's Brewery, one of whose entrances is known as St James's Gate. Even more important, the gate was the traditional starting point for the still-alive Camino de Santiago de Compostela (the Pilgrimage of St James of Compostela) to northern Spain. Following the hospital name change to St James's, the then less than salubrious institution embarked on a long term project to make it the biggest and best in the state.

The logo for the thriving new hospital was a mystery to me, even though I had been involved in the design of logos for a couple of emerging organisations. It seemed fussy, detached from the clarity of design characteristic of the time, and somewhat unimaginative. On the surface it suggested a bureaucratically overburdened county council or one of the old health boards. However, when looked at carefully, it yielded up more and created an immediate link with the history of the area and the life of the community out of which it had emerged. The logo draws on the symbolism of the scallop shell which is used to mark the Camino pilgrims' walking trails all over Europe, as they converge on Santiago de Compostela. It

draws on the hospital's proximity to St James's Gate and associates it with the universal human aspiration the Camino has
come to represent. The significance of the logo was a sleeper
in the hospital for a generation after its modern recreation.

I was a 'friend' on Pat's Facebook, and at that time he regularly posted interesting and challenging material. Around the
end of 2014 he left a message requesting that I contact him
and I did so promptly. He had a difficulty that he could not
get a foothold on and thought I might be able to help. The
problem arose from clearing the areas on site necessary for
the new project. This involved demolition of buildings as well
as moving the occupants and relocating some departments.
John B. Keane's play *The Field* gives an idea of the type of ter-
ritorial transactions that had to take place, and the determi-
nation necessary to find good solutions to hard won and hard
held positions. But in St James's people were accustomed to
this, as rolling development of the site had been ongoing for
over a quarter of a century. Nevertheless, it was difficult and
dirty work, both figuratively and literally. No effort was spared
to keep things moving, and a large area at the South Circular
Road end of the campus was completely cleared of the existing buildings, including a whole hospital block, a private
clinic, several big departments including the department of
which I had been head, and the hospital chapel. Initially, I
suspected the CEO's problem might arise from intransigence
in my old department, but this was not so.

The problem was the Catholic chapel, which was the only
one on site. Its imminent demolition was complicated by
the fact that the planning for its replacement had escaped
the attention of senior management. A potentially divisive

'solution' emerged without board approval and had innocently gathered momentum. The culture of the hospital and its board was vigorously secular, and sensitive to its location in the city which had strong Jewish and Muslim associations. The board shared the fashionable antipathy of the times to the 'Faith of our Fathers'. In addition, a large proportion of the nurses and many of the doctors were of Asian origin with corresponding religious affiliations.

I listened to his analysis, and immediately recognised, as a former attender at the hospital board, the bear pit he was about to enter. He felt that I had an involvement with secular spiritualities after retirement, and this might help fashion an approach that could find broad acceptance.

∞   ∞   ∞

An initiative to solve the problem of replacing the chapel had been well underway; busy people got on with it and kept up the momentum without the CEO or board getting directly involved. A budget of about one million euro was agreed and the director of buildings arranged for it to be designed and built on the assumption this was what was needed to replace the chapel. The new chapel was prominently located in an area that opened onto the main hospital foyer. To understand this happening without board and senior management involvement, it is necessary to realise that St James's is as big as a medium-sized town and many large and small building projects are ongoing all the time. They seldom attract much attention and the distraction of site clearance exacerbated this.

Meetings of the interested parties were convened by the CEO, and included the director of buildings, the head chaplain, an atheist board member, Fran Hegarty (chairman of the arts committee), and the architect responsible for the new St James's. Sensitivities in the hospital board about religious matters were highlighted. I felt for Pat, who was going to have to inform the board that it was the owner of a new chapel it did not know about, and what is more, it opened on to the main foyer of the hospital. The record of the board included instructing that a Christmas Crib constructed in the foyer be taken down. So, it had form. In addition, most of those at the meeting had problems of one sort or another with the new building. There were unresolved issues about how it should be furnished, about the acoustics which were not satisfactory, about the artwork to be incorporated, and how it should be named.

The chaplains were proceeding on the reasonable assumption that the new building, which they felt was replacing a Catholic Church, would also be one. However, it was quickly accepted that this was unlikely to be agreed by the board, and a decision to revisit the purpose and scope of the new building was taken. All accepted that it should not favour any one denomination, and that all denominations/religions as well as none should be welcome there. We agreed to revisit the decoration, furnishing, artwork, purpose and involvement of different churches and religions. The head chaplain co-operated generously with this, but one suspects he may have been under some pressure from his own constituency. The Chief Rabbi and local Imam were invited to participate, and I was asked to assist with defining a way forward that would be acceptable to the various religious, secular and spiritual sensibilities involved.

The following weeks saw much discussion and exploration of possible solutions. Initially, we were hopeful that an approach based on the artwork to be commissioned might offer a solution. With Fran Hegarty, we considered small chapels that had become places of pilgrimage for people of all denominations and none, like the Rothko chapel in Houston, Texas, or the beautiful chapel atheist Henri Matisse designed and decorated for the Dominican nuns in Vence in the south of France. While travelling at that time, I looked at multifaith chapels in hospitals, airports and universities, but found only one that really commended itself: the new Faith Centre at the London School of Economics. It is a relatively small but stunning collection of spaces on one floor of a large new building. The capacity of the largest space is about 100. It is decorated inexpensively in bright primary colours and used by Christian, Muslim, Jewish and secular groups. However, it became clear that while these ideas had potential in the long term, a more urgent resolution was required.

Much discouraged, I decided to stop researching what we might emulate, and headed to the Canaries for a break. Nothing happened for a while, but then the solution emerged in an unlikely way, as it often does in these situations. Walking the Atlantic shore one evening, I decided to buy *The Irish Times*, which was still available there at the time. Paging through it, I happened on an article on the Camino. It emphasised the participation of those from all faiths and none, and that those who did so enjoyed a sense of personal or spiritual renewal through participation. The article described the small oratories/churches along the route that pilgrims could rest in, often known as a Camino Rest. So here was a solution: the building would not be a chapel, it would be a *Camino Rest*. And what could be more appropriate in a hospital with a logo derived from the Camino, and whose name is a translation of its destination.

And so it happened on return, with much to and fro, with long discussion among colleagues, support was built for the proposal, and enthusiasm grew for an idea rooted in the closeness of the hospital to St James's Gate and its historical significance for the city. Members of the working group warmed to the idea, refined and nuanced it, and were energised by it. The CEO fostered it and brought it back and forth to the board. The chaplains, the Imam et al. were happy and the purpose and arrangements for the new building were defined around this concept. The board, though initially cautious, enthusiastically adopted it. A special service was devised, and following a procession from the old chapel, The Camino Rest was dedicated in an inclusive moving ceremony that all the stakeholders could live with and most were enthusiastic about.

A large welcoming notice at the end of the main hospital foyer now reads:

> **Camino Rest:** *serves as a house of prayer, a sacred and quiet space for people of all faith traditions and also for those who express no spiritual preference or faith. It is a sanctuary where patients, visitors and staff can rest, reflect and refresh themselves through prayer, meditation or other accepted forms of personal renewal.*

It was an inclusive outcome to what had the potential to become divisive or exclusive. It was rewarding to be part of helping Pat Plunkett as CEO and the hospital team. For me, there is a wonderful silent symmetry and reciprocity about his invaluable and equally silent help with the bishop's dilemma described earlier. And now both stories are, at least partly, told.

Chapter Eleven

Come Dance with Me in Ireland!

True ease in writing comes from Art, not Chance,
As those move easiest who have learn'd to dance.

– Alexander Pope

On November 13, 2018, two days after President Higgins was inaugurated for his second term, I sat on the west-facing Las Canteras beach of Las Palmas city in Gran Canaria, mesmerised by the unquenchable energy of the surfer-bearing Atlantic breakers. It was just after lunch, and in deference to the health puritans, I had walked about a mile. So, lulled by exercise, food and a pleasant temperature in the low twenties, I lapsed into digesting and ruminating. President Higgins' inaugural speech was challenging and seemed to nudge us toward more inclusiveness and empathy in public life. I couldn't remember anything so vividly from the inaugural speeches of his predecessors, Presidents Robinson and McAleese, who flanked him during the speech. President McAleese, to his left, looked distinguished, if a little frayed. President Robinson, on the other hand, looked just like her more recent slightly unkempt self, and was dressed in an outfit an African chief might have felt at home in. It was difficult to associate her with the only sentence I remember from her inaugural speech: *I am of Ireland. Come dance with me in Ireland.*

The invitation is from a W.B. Yeats poem 'I am of Ireland'. The full line is a refrain that ends many of the verses and is attributed to a fourteenth century Irish poet. All things considered, it seemed then and even more so now an unlikely quote for Mrs Robinson to work into her speech. Perhaps it was intended to reflect something exciting and disruptive in Irish identity. It created a striking image, stronger than the individual words suggest, had great traction with the public, both in Ireland and internationally, and in some respects paved the way for *Riverdance*. Within Ireland, set dancers, sean nós dancers and even céilí dancers embraced it.

The revival of set dancing was well underway by the time of the presidential invitation. It had become a popular, heady movement during the 1980s and into the 1990s and, for a while, was regarded as a trendy activity. This was helped by the extent of the media attention it attracted, and its being integrated into the then widely reported Merriman Summer School. Many well-known personalities of the day like David Hanley, Nell McCafferty and Nuala O'Faolain gave it a good airing. Among the artefacts produced in the set dancing community was a small lapel badge with two figures dancing and the invitation surrounding them in text. I bought several, and often wore them to set dancing events as well as on trips abroad, where they were an easy icebreaker for conversation. There was also a growing network of set dancing clubs and events in many cities in the UK, Europe, the US and even in parts of Asia. The invitation predates *Riverdance* by about five years, and so was rooted in tradition and not a response to a fad or something that became trendy in the 1990s.

I never danced with Mrs Robinson but reckon if her speech delivery is anything to go by she might be a wooden and somewhat unpredictable dancer. In fact, it is possible that she might even be dangerous and leave a stream of collisional dancing injuries in her wake. As an experienced dancer, I could tell a lot about a person's disposition and some aspects of their physical health by dancing with them for a few minutes. For example, it was very easy to sense somebody who was tense or nervous but, perhaps more surprising, I could guestimate the adequacy or otherwise of a partner's bone mineral status, with a little help from physics and a consideration of angular momentum.

In late 1990 or early 1991, some weeks after Mary Robinson's speech, I attended a weekend set dancing[3] session in Ennis, County Clare, and as winter had set in sought accommodation in the town to avoid a drive to and from the coast. The town was full, but I eventually secured a place in a B&B not far from the O'Connell monument in the centre. The programme included a fantastic Saturday night sets event with live music and contributions of song and dance from star performers among the attendees.

---

[3] Irish sets are danced as quadrilles with four couples opposite each other in square format. Some of the sets have structure and movements seen in European and military dances. The Irish versions are greatly energised by use of local music and the stepping for reels, jigs, polkas, slides, and hornpipes. They are very sociable, and one dances closely with a partner. This was regarded as too intimate, and the céilí dances which will be more familiar to many from schooldays were invented to offset this problem. The sets were common in house-dances in many counties. Each area tended to have its own variation in both form and stepping.

At breakfast in the B&B on Sunday morning, it was clear that most of the clientele were dancers. A rather severe matronly woman presided, providing tea or coffee, and the full Irish, to all in the unequivocally domestic setting of her breakfast room. The tables were close to each other, and a solitary male at an adjacent table struck up a conversation with me.

'Great that the president is supporting the dancing. I suppose she might shake a leg herself someday,' he said.

'You'd never know. Where do you come from?' He had a Clare accent, and I was curious.

'From out the road near Corofin.'

'Great music and dancing out that way,' I replied.

'Mighty!' He said, and finishing off his coffee, he wiped his lips with the serviette and stood up. 'I'll take a coffee up to herself and save her the trouble of coming down. A great breed, *Mná na hEireann* (The Women of Ireland).'

And with that, the room settled down and he departed, accompanied by a hostile glare from our presiding host.

'Hmph,' she snorted from her matronly service corner, making sure the whole room could hear. 'I'll give him Mná na hEireann. And he up in the room with that trollop, and the wife out in Corofin, thinking he's doing something useful. Come dance with me in Ireland – how are you? I'll give him Mná na hEireann.'

She flounced out, and I still wonder what followed. The dancing community in Clare is generally less judgemental. Perhaps it's just as well as dancing is sometimes thought of as a vertical expression of a horizontal desire.

At the best set dancing venues in West Clare, some evidence that this might be the case could be found by the discerning observer. On a cold winter evening, at one such venue, it quickly warmed up once the dancing got going. As might be expected, some of the dancers respond with an uncomfortable excess of sweating, and many of both sexes bring clothing changes with them. The changes and freshening up are generally discreet, happen quickly in the breaks between dances, often in the unheated toilets of parish or school/community halls. I recall, on a freezing night, going to change my shirt and on entering the toilet, encountering the vision of a strong muscular man in his forties with steam rising from his body as one occasionally sees with racehorses. Memorable and visceral.

∞ ∞ ∞

Vaughan's Barn in Kilfenora was among the best set dancing venues. I was a patron there for many years, and here is the story of an evening early in the new century. On the night in question, there were too many cars to park along the road so, as locals do, I slipped in through their farmyard gate and found a vacant spot not submerged in mud. It was about 9.45 pm and the late summer evening was still bright and a little sultry. The air mixed benign farmyard and Atlantic salt, not quite bracing but not high summer humidity.

Entering the subdued daylight of the barn, the part of the pub reserved for set dancing, was strange. But it quickly regained its familiarity, the smell of Guinness spiking authentic Atlantic damp. It is a long narrow room, like the side aisle of a small church. All kinds of artefacts were suspended from the pitched roof including an old bicycle, a pair of very large boots, and numerous kitchen utensils all garnished with a generous coating of last year's dust. The bar at the end of the room had a cluster of people chatting and laughing amiably. Small clusters of people throughout the room created an air of anticipation as did the musicians, known as the Four

Courts. Sometimes there were five or six in the Four Courts, and occasionally as few as three had to suffice. This evening they were four middle aged men, animated and chatting with the people around them. I got a drink and walked toward the musicians, old friends.

And then I noticed her, a solitary figure about halfway up the room sitting to one side reading a guidebook about the region. Where had I met her? It came back to me: at a conference, a German doctor in her forties, who during one of the social functions had explained how difficult holidays were for single people. And I had told her about this part of the world. I greeted her, disguising surprise that she was there. She seemed a little disappointed at the damp, the salt encrusted windows and the dust, none in keeping with German window hygiene.

'Hello Sylvia, what a surprise to see you here.' She looked up from her book, stood to greet me, and said:

'I wondered if you would be here. I took your advice and am going to the summer school you recommended next week but decided to come a few days early and look around. When did you arrive?'

'I left work in Dublin this afternoon and have only just arrived. But, as I probably told you, this is a regular stopping point for me. And I'll be at the summer school all next week also, but unfortunately have homework to do for it before the weekend. Have you had a chance to see much of the area?'

'Oh,' she replied. 'I have been looking at the megalithic tombs and the Celtic high crosses. After dinner in the main pub this evening, I walked to the cathedral ruin to see the Doorty Cross. It is so well preserved after so many centuries and its surroundings look so well cared for.'

'Well,' I said, 'Would you like to meet the person that looks after it?'

Mary Doorty had just come in and was saying hello to people right and left. I greeted her with a warm embrace and introduced her to Sylvia. She welcomed her enthusiastically and she proudly explained that this high cross had been the responsibility of her late husband's family for centuries. Mary is full of enthusiasm and though on the wrong side of 70 she not only danced with enthusiasm but was skilful and never short of a partner. I'd known her for years and when we were both in the barn, we often gave each other the first dance of the evening.

'Come on,' Mary said. 'It's time to get these musicians going and then we can have our dance.'

And she departed in a flurry to find the MC and signalled to the musicians that she was on their case. Sylvia watched her with something between disbelief and incomprehension, and I began to realise that I might be part of an emerging social problem. But, I reminded myself, a good dancing partner is harder to get than a wife.

'When does the dancing start anyway?' Sylvia enquired. 'It says 9.00 pm on the notice outside.'

'Oh, don't pay any attention to that,' I said. 'It actually starts when the musicians and MC are ready, and that is surprisingly constant in the summer, a Germanic 9.54 pm.'

She wasn't impressed. She looked about with lack of enthusiasm at the archaeological quantities of dust and men whose dress would be well adapted to a night of football training or delivering a calf in an open field. She could barely contain an urge to find a serviette and tackle the windows.

To distract her I said: 'Would you like to dance, or would you prefer to watch for a while?'

'Oh,' she said, 'I might as well jump in at the start.'

The musicians had taken their places and the people were drifting onto the floor and forming themselves into sets. Mary nodded across the floor indicating that she had booked a place for us in one of the sets. In this type of dancing, the experienced know that getting a place in a set is more important than getting a partner. If you have a place, you will always get a partner, but not vice versa.

How to handle all this, and what to do about Sylvia, I wondered. Quick decisive action was needed. I took her hand and guided her to a set with a gap in it and told her to stand there and not to panic; I would find a partner for her. This is not difficult in the barn. It is accustomed to visitors and good dancers were always willing to lead somebody new who wished to dance. I found just the man. We'll call him 'Taffy Tommy'. He was a great dancer and a teacher, and was sitting to one side intending to pass for this dance, but he graciously obliged. I quickly introduced him to Sylvia; she looked anxious, not sure what to make of him or what she was letting herself in for. I slipped away quickly and made for the other set with Mary just as the MC announced the first dance of the evening. Fifteen minutes to figure out what to do.

After the first dance, I went to see how she got on. She was glowing with excitement and achievement.

'Will you have a drink?' I asked.

'Oh yes!'

I started to go to the bar and she quickly intercepted me.

'But will there be time?' she enquired. 'One of the other men in the set I was in asked me to dance the next one with him. Will I be able to have a drink before that?' She was anxious.

'No,' I replied, 'but I'll get you one anyway, and I'll make it a large glass of water with ice. You'll need it if you dance two sets on the trot. And will you save the set after the next one for me?'

'Of course,' she said, and I headed to the bar while she was picked up by her new partner for the second dance.

The night passed quickly and three hours later she was overwhelmed with exhaustion and high on extraordinary music and dancing and its power to bind people together. Her elegant outfit was drenched and sweat stained, and it is safe to assume she had forgotten about dust and salt encrusted windows. I suspect she might have revised her earlier judgment on the dress sense of the men she danced with. She'd had a new experience that felt special and I mused that the following week might prove less of a problem than I feared.

I was a late vocation to set dancing, and my first introduction to it was through Brook's Acdemy, and the teaching of Mary Friel, Irene Martin and Eileen O'Doherty (Chapter Three). My father never danced, except once under duress at a wedding. Presumably, out of loyalty to him, mother never danced much when he was alive. Soon after he died in 1990, she took an interest in seeing sets danced at the Willie Clancy Summer School (Chapter Three). She soon graduated to attending workshops at which the sets were taught, both in Milltown and in Dublin. Thereafter, she danced regularly until a decline in health during her eighties excluded it. There is something special about dancing with your mother, and perhaps dancing with one's daughter is also special. I feel privileged to have enjoyed both during those years.

During one of the Willie Clancy Schools, my mother told me excitedly that she had seen the same set they used to dance 60 years before in Brosna, reconstructed at the evening concert. It had died out and possibly had not been danced much, if at all, for 50 of those 60 years. In many parts of the country, the now infamous Dance Halls Act of the 1930s, combined with unsympathetic clerical and financial influences, virtually eliminated the sets. However, they survived in Clare and some other counties. During the 1980s and 1990s the decline was reversed during the revival, which owed a great deal to Connie Ryan, about whom more later.

The Willie Clancy Concerts were, like coarse wholemeal brown bread, something special. They were hastily thrown together in the community hall every evening during the summer school. Each had a different theme and one evening was always given over to dance. Most, if not all, of the relevant artists and musicians contributed. Many were well known nationally and/or internationally and gave their services *pro bono,* but may have been exempted from the modest registration fee or granted a night or two of accommodation. The shows were rough and ready, and not produced in any formal sense, but the artists present gave of their best. Curation of the whole enterprise was somewhat random with no discernible rationale to the sequence of presentations, other than practical availability and some deference to a well understood seniority among performers who had weathered the day during harder times. There was no knowing when the concerts would end: some lasted two hours and a few, I recall, went to four and a half. In retrospect, they were extraordinary events, with most of the artists leaving the audience to perform two or three short pieces and then rejoining the audience.

The audience, a phenomenon in its own right, drew people together from all walks of life. They ranged from very scruffy (and smelly) campers to suited visitors including politicians, senior clerics, diplomats, academics, media people and Comháltas officials. Many had (sometimes bored) children in tow, and if the weather was wet, the hall quickly took on the vaguely humid and fetid atmosphere of the upper deck of a Dublin bus during rush hour.

Despite all of this, the music, unaccompanied singing, and the dancing were exceptional, inspired and sometimes visceral. They were in the best Clare traditions, not tamed or tarnished by clerical or official interference during the preceding decades. Many in the audience brought recording devices in the hope of capturing some of the many special moments that most years brought. I never tried this approach, and indeed also seldom took photographs. Both distract and take from the special moments, which can only be savoured then and there, and possibly in memory.

I often reflect on the thousands of tapes and discs that must rest on shelves in thousands of homes right across the globe. Are they listened to? If so, do the listeners notice the barking of the dog in the garden adjacent to the parish hall? Every night for the decade or more that I attended these concerts the performers were accompanied, at some time in the evening, by the dog's relentless barking. Nevertheless, the show went on and somehow the psyche filtered out the barking during special moments, even if it was present at other times. And we, both performers and audience, enjoyed a (non-pharmacological) high through being gathered together in a small village hall on the edge of the Atlantic, in the gradually fading light of magical July evenings.

Connie Ryan (mentioned above) was an exceptional and charismatic Dance Master at the heart of the set dance revival. A medium height, stocky and well-built man, he was devoted to researching and passing on the almost moribund tradition. Raised in Tipperary, he lost most of his sight in a hurling accident while still young. In many ways he was untutored but had an unerring instinct for what was important and worthwhile in life, and this more than compensated for any deficit in education or loss of visual acuity. He had an exceptional ease with people from all levels in society and all walks of life, and had an irreverent, ebullient sense of humour that knew few, if any, boundaries. In teaching and general demeanour, he had a rumbustiousness that didn't allow for pomposity, and gatherings in his company were inevitably experienced as occasions in which rank, or position, had no importance.

Connie taught experientially, building up the various elements of knowledge and skill the participants at workshops needed. Some express surprise that a partially sighted man could research and teach dance. For example, to read the time, he had to raise his arm so that it was directly in front of his face, and the watch was less than six inches from his eyes. Despite this he was a stickler for punctuality,

'I start on time and I finish on time,' he firmly impressed on workshops.

Yet despite his handicap, he was able to sense movement, grace and style. He could sense workshop participants who were struggling, and would stand near the set they were dancing in. His solution was to approach them, often with a humorous comment:

'It's your left foot, toe – heel – toe,' he would say.

'No – not that left foot – it's the other left foot, the one at the end of your left leg.'

Then, if the participant was really struggling, Connie would embrace them, man or woman, very close and tightly, and dance out the piece that had been going astray, with wonderful stepping and precision. This had an extraordinary effect, as you sensed throughout your full body exactly what the rhythm and step should feel like and, thus, could recognise it once it gradually began to come right. Dancing to him was obviously not a spectator sport or an academic pursuit; it was an immersive experience.

By the end of his career, he had workshops almost every weekend in some part of the country, or in one of many cities in the UK, Europe or the US. He died before his time in May 1997, taken after a two-year battle with colon cancer, during which he made all the arrangements for his funeral in Tipperary. These included some figures of the Plain Set (which was normally the last dance of an evening) to be danced behind the hearse before it moved off from the church, and a graveyard oration by Diarmuid Breathnach, Chairman of Cumman Merriman. Commenting on Connie's life, work and his capacity to inspire people and make them laugh, Diarmuid said to the huge crowd gathered in the cemetery:

> ... he help[ed] us all rediscover in ourselves something which suburbia, and perhaps stress, are near to destroying, that sense of merriment and of joy which we associate more readily with, say, school children released from the classroom. And ... Connie had the means to create merriment, set dancing.... Like children, it was ourselves we were applauding as soon as we had barely learned ... a set. We had been caught unawares. Something of our essential selves was laid bare. At dancing sessions Connie divested us of all the trappings of class, status, bias, age or whatever... [His] was the sort of miracle which Ireland badly needed but did not entirely deserve.

∞   ∞   ∞

Indeed, we did not fully appreciate or deserve him. Many who contributed much less to Irish life and culture have been recognised in various ways, including the award of an honorary degree by one of the universities. Connie would have been a worthy recipient of one, and it is a shame that we did not take the opportunity to do so while he was still with us. But he is well remembered in other ways. A year after his death, a special memorial function was organised to celebrate his memory, in his home place in Clonoulty, County Tipperary. It drew a sufficiently large crowd to warrant hiring a marquee big enough to take a Dublin 4 socialite wedding. The programme included a dance workshop.

For more than a decade prior to this I had a wonderful dancing partner, Máire Ní Iarnáin, from the Aran Islands. We both knew Connie well, so this was an unmissable event. We had learned much from him and had greatly enjoyed his company and his approach to dance, life and the universe. Máire is an elegant, slightly built person, and dances with exceptional grace. We came to dance together in a strange way, based on shared experiences of illnesses. She, at age 40, had a hip replacement, and I had chronic back problems. We found we could dance freely together knowing with confidence that we were both alert to and skilled in avoiding dancing injuries without cramping style.

The pilgrimage to Connie's place occurred in the context of an additional health problem on my part. I'd suffered a heart attack months earlier and had been grounded from both dancing and work up to that point. I still felt like an invalid but had started taking trips out. For example, I attended hearings of the then current planning tribunal in Dublin Castle, which with the infamous, James (Will we f**k!) Gogarty as a witness, was the best free entertainment in town. However, walking up to and back from the castle was a slow affair. Nevertheless, Máire visited me and from time to time got me to dance around the kitchen in a low-key way. In retrospect, I think how kind and attentive she was. So, we resolved to go to Connie's function, and agreed I could sit out the dancing and watch.

The weather was splendid, and the marque looked like an oasis shimmering in the sun. A couple of hundred people or more circulated freely to a background of Irish music, and it was a pleasure to meet many who I had not seen for a while. After the formalities our mentors for the day, Pat Murphy, established dance master, and Betty McCoy, Connie's business and dancing partner, called the workshop to order. They explained they would work on several sets, and I settled down to watch with Máire chatting animatedly beside me.

'Gosh,' she said. 'What a crowd. There's well over 200 here. Will there be room for all the sets?'

'I'd say a lot might be local dignitaries and family, but still there are enough dancers for over twenty sets. And a few are hungover, so they'll be sitting for a while,' I replied.

'There'll be lots of room. Now! We'll find a nice chair for you with a good view, and you'll be able to keep an eye on all the scandal.'

'You should dance,' I said and pointed to a few people in the crowd she might like to dance with.

'No. I'm going to sit here and keep an eye on you.'

With that, attention moved to the centre of the floor where Pat and Betty were standing with microphones and encouraging the crowd to move back and free up space in the centre of the dance floor. At workshops like this, it is customary for the dance master to invite experienced dancers to help demonstrate various figures and steps so that the participants can visualise what the set should look like. Our hosts glanced around the room searching for likely demonstrators and Pat caught Máire's eye.

'Máire and Jim,' he announced over the public address system. 'Will you demonstrate?'

I blanched, and looked up at her, mouthing, 'NO.' She shook her head in Pat's direction. But people frequently refused in the politely understated Irish way, just as they might initially refuse a drink or a second helping at a meal.

'Come out here now,' he commanded, pointing to a spot in the centre of the floor. 'Connie would want you to do it.'

The only valid excuse at this stage would have been a severe hangover or a letter from the gynaecologist. Máire looked down and said:

'Come on – it'll be okay. We'll take it handy – no more than dancing around the kitchen.'

With some trepidation, I got up, and we went to the centre of the room while three other couples were being similarly *volunteered*.

∞   ∞   ∞

We walked through the movements of the first figure of the set several times, something we knew well and got through without mistakes. But Pat signalled for the music to start, and lively Clare reels filled the marquee. I was gripped by a mixture of a desire to dance and fear of what could happen when I did so. We danced the figure – about three minutes in total. The sky didn't fall! The finer points of the figure were walked through again, and we danced it again and, although winded, my trepidation was being replaced by a surge of something much more positive. We returned to our seats at the edge of the floor, while the participants sorted themselves into sets and walked through and then danced what we had just demonstrated.

Then we were called on to demonstrate the second figure. The break had been long enough for trepidation to re-establish itself, but it quickly dissipated. Time passed quickly, and in the two and a half hours we had demonstrated all six figures. Máire was smiling, and so was I; dance might be back on the agenda earlier than expected. My mood had moved from apprehension and trepidation to elation, and in retrospect this was the day when I ceased being a coddled, cautious invalid and returned to the world of the well. And all because of an accidental invitation to demonstrate a dance – it was a lot less expensive than a consultation with a cardiologist.

Years later, I had lunch with one of our mentors from that day, Betty McCoy, and recalled my quasi-miraculous recovery and how she had contributed to it. She was deeply moved and had no sense of this happening at the time. On the other hand, with the benefit of distance and hindsight, I sometimes wonder if there might have been a little collusion between Pat (or herself) and Máire, with a view to halting my malingering. Either way, I look back on the occasion with gratitude and appreciation.

Máire and I continued to dance for a further ten years, and often demonstrated sets for groups at home and abroad. She danced with lightness, grace and style and, though slight of figure, about halfway through that period needed her bad hip replaced a second time. With fortitude, she fought the problems of regaining mobility and muscle control and I was privileged to be able to help her back to dancing, as she had done years earlier for me.

Eventually, all good things come to an end and so it was with this. Further health problems conspired to make it impossible for me to continue, and with great regret I had to retire from this life-enhancing activity. Now, after a long period, many of the problems are gone or greatly reduced. Cardiac issues seem to have moved into the background and arthritic shoulders, feet, and ankles have been rendered less of a problem by the ministry of surgeons and pain physicians.

Should I try it again now? Wishful thinking or something for a lengthening bucket list? I'll phone Máire and see how she is.

Acknowledgements

I am grateful to family members and professional colleagues who have, sometimes unwittingly, contributed to these *Tales*. As they read, they may recognise themselves, but they may also escape recognition. David Givens, the Publisher, has a way with advice born of a deep, incisive, honest experience. He is usually right, even when he is wrong. Thank you, David, for making what can be a troubled experience into an almost painless pleasure.

I am grateful to the founding Trustees of the Robert Boyle Foundation, J. Kieran Taaffe (Chairman) RIP, Tim Lyne (Secretary), and Davis Coakley RIP for their endless support, guidance, validation and encouragement for over twenty years (see also Preface). Many of the tales depend on this and it is continued by the current Trustees including Patricia Egan (Chairman), Tim Lyne (Secretary), Fran Hegarty, Paddy Gilligan, Barry McMahon and Tanya Kenny.

Many friends and colleagues read parts of the manuscript and offered suggestions and encouragement. They include Mary Coffey, Steve Ebdon Jackson, Kevin Egan, Michael Hanna, Odile Hendricks, Ola Holmberg, John McEvoy, Iggy McGovern, Pat Plunkett, Una Quinn and Christina Skourou. I often brought extracts to the meetings of the Trinity

Retirement Association's writing group. The members, including Pat Wall, Tim Jackson, Rose Kevany, Mary McCarthy, Sara McMurry, Eamon O'Driscoll, Yvonne Scannelli, and Eamon Sweeney, were never less than kind and encouraging. They gently nudged the work in directions it might not have otherwise taken and improved it. In a different vein, thanks to Cara McEvoy of 18 Words for her rapid and assured language and English usage edit.

At a different level, I will be eternally grateful (should promises re that time span prove dependable) to those who provided the context in which the *Tales* came about. They had the difficult task of managing a professional life crisscrossing the boundary between the Ivory Tower and the health sector. They did so with creativity, imagination and a willingness to indulge my excesses of enthusiasm. This, among other things, allowed physics to be brought into the health service in a way that needed to happen but remained to be achieved in the last quarter of the twentieth century. To do so, they had to resist failures of imagination in government departments. Those involved include Liam Dunbar, John O'Brien, Desmond Dempsey and Tim Lyne, successive CEOs of St James's Hospital and Federated Dublin Voluntary Hospitals; Professors Dermot Hourihane, John Bonner, Ian Temperley and Davis Coakley, successive Deans of the School of Medicine in TCD; Professor George Sevastopulo, Dean of Graduate Studies at TCD; Dr Gerry Hurley, Dean of the Faculty of Radiology at the RCSI, Drs David Legge and Ned Malone of the same parish; and Drs Bill Watts and Tom Mitchell, successive Provosts of TCD. Their combined efforts created a unique role that became an effective instrument of change and was unremittingly satisfying to occupy.

Acknowledgements

The following sources of quoted material are gratefully acknowledged. All fall within the rubric of fair usage. Wendy Cope's poem 'Bloody Men' in *Serious Concerns* (Faber and Faber). Emanuel Kant's tombstone. Seamus Heaney's poem 'Postscript' from his collection *The Spirit Level* (Faber and Faber) and a quote from his Nobel Prize Lecture. Frank O'Connor's *The Midnight Court* (The O'Brien Press). Ciaran Carson's *The Midnight Court* (Gallery Books). Alexander Pope's 'An Essay in Criticism' and his 'Essay on Man, Epistle II'. Jenny Diski in her book *Why Didn't You Just Do What You Were Told?* (Bloomsbury). Robertson Davies in *The Cornish Trilogy* (Penguin Books). Teilhard de Chardin in *Le Milieu Divin* (Fontana Books). Michael D. Higgins, for an Irish language proverb frequently quoted. Sinead Morrissey in her collection *Parallax: And Selected Poems* (Farrar, Strauss & Giroux). Derek Mahon, for a quote attributed to him that is a variant of one often attributed to Albert Einstein. Alan Bennett, from the introduction to *Talking Heads* (1988, Faber and Faber, and BBC). Edward Hopper in his 'Notes on Painting' for his 1933 exhibition at the Museum of Modern Art (MOMA, New York). Image/paintings credits are noted in the colour inserts.